D1626067

CELTIC ORNAMENT

CELTIC ORNAMENT

IN THE BRITISH ISLES

DOWN TO A.D. 700

BY

E. T. LEEDS, M.A., F.S.A.

Keeper of the Ashmolean Museum
Oxford

WITHDRAWN

OXFORD
AT THE CLARENDON PRESS
1933

OXFORD
UNIVERSITY PRESS
AMEN HOUSE, E.C. 4
London Edinburgh Glasgow
Leipzig New York Toronto
Melbourne Capetown Bombay
Calcutta Madras Shanghai
HUMPHREY MILFORD
PUBLISHER TO THE
UNIVERSITY

PRINTED IN GREAT BRITAIN

PREFACE

THIS little book is the outcome of a lecture delivered to the first meeting of the International Congress of Prehistoric and Protohistoric Sciences held in London in August, 1932. It has been considerably expanded from the form in which it was actually delivered, though the general lines of the argument remain as before. Its compilation would have been impossible save for the very real assistance received from many quarters, by facilities accorded for the study of collections, by the supply of photographs or casts, and by personal correspondence. I would mention more particularly the authorities of the Departments of British Antiquities and of Coins and Medals in the British Museum; the Keeper of the National Museum of Scottish Antiquities in Edinburgh, the Keeper of Irish Antiquities in the National Museum in Dublin, and the Curators of the Museums at Liverpool, Colchester, and Belfast.

To the Trustees of the British Museum I am indebted for permission to reproduce Figs. 7, 16, and 18; to Librairie E. Leroux, Paris, for Fig. 6; to the Council of the Society of Antiquaries of London for the use of Figs. 1, 9, 12, 14, 19, 23(*b*), 27, 29(*a*), and 35(*b*); to the Council of the Society of Antiquaries of Scotland for the use of Figs. 4, 17, 25, 32, 34, and 35*a*; to the Council of the Cambrian Archaeological Association for Fig. 22; and to the Royal Archaeological Institute of Great Britain and Ireland for Figs. 11 and 23(*a*).

Thanks are specially due to the Delegates of the University Press, Oxford, for undertaking the publication

of the book and to the Staff of the Press for the interest
they have taken in its production.

Finally, I would wish to record the particular obli-
gation under which I stand to my friends, Mr. T. D.
Kendrick and Miss M. V. Taylor, for much information
placed at my disposal, and above all to Mr. R. G. Collingwood, who read the manuscript and offered many
valuable criticisms and suggestions.

E. T. L.

CONTENTS

LIST OF ILLUSTRATIONS

COLOURED PLATES

INTRODUCTION

IT is over thirty-five years ago that Mr. (now Sir) Arthur Evans chose as the subject for the Rhind Lectures a survey of Celtic Art. Unfortunately the delivery of those lectures almost coincided with the initiation of his activities in that field of Aegean archaeological research with which his name will be always intimately associated, with the result that his Rhind Lectures were never published in extended form. But, as the summary issued to those who attended his lectures indicates, they would, following as they did on such preliminary studies as the account of the Aesica brooch, the publication of the Aylesford cemetery, and the description of the votive hoard from North Ireland, undoubtedly have set the study of Celtic art on the right path, by their full appreciation of the various factors underlying the development of that art throughout its existence. Time would have brought in its train modifications of certain details, but the broad outlines envisaged in those lectures would have remained as an invaluable basis for all future investigation.

The blank left in the archaeological literature of this country by the omission to give those lectures to a larger world fell to another to endeavour to fill. The outcome of that endeavour was J. Romilly Allen's *Celtic Art in Pagan and Pre-Christian Times*, published in 1904, itself an expansion of various articles in *Archaeologia Cambrensis* and other journals, and this has remained the standard work on the subject since its appearance.

The author states in the first sentence of his preface that 'the book is an attempt to give a concise summary of the facts at present available for forming a theory of the origin and development of Celtic Art in Great Britain and Ireland', and no one will deny that it furnished the student with a conspectus of the large and valuable body of material scattered among the collections in museums and an extensive archaeological literature, while at the same time it treated the development of that art in a new and original fashion.

But at the present day knowledge of the Celts and their art has been immensely advanced. It might even be held that much that Romilly Allen included under the epithet of Celtic would now no longer be readily accepted as such. For, even though there may be a general consensus of opinion that Celts in some form or another were already installed in this country during the Bronze Age, there would be great hesitation in tracing back the origins of the art of even this pre-Iron Age element to the sources from which he derived them.

Romilly Allen's work was particularly notable for the masterly ingenuity which he brought to bear on the interpretation of the technical methods employed in the construction of the interlaced work on monuments of the Christian period, and to a lesser extent of the designs of the pre-Christian age. But, especially in regard to the latter, his work almost entirely failed to grasp the historical side of the development, and any one with even a moderate knowledge of the subject will at once detect the commingling in his pages of material separated often by several centuries.

Valuable rectifications of this neglect of the historical method have since been provided, particularly by the *British Museum Guide to the Antiquities of the Iron Age* compiled by Mr. R. A. Smith, as also others in which

descriptions with a more regional application are pre-
faced by remarks of a general character. But by the
very nature of the limitations of the material with which
these had to deal, a survey of the whole field was for
them obviously impossible.

The present work is, like Romilly Allen's, an attempt,
but smaller in compass. It essays no more than to sketch
the lines along which the study of pre-Christian Celtic
Ornament as it is known in Britain should be directed:
its origins are barely touched upon, except in so far as
is necessary to emphasize the differences engendered by
transplantation to, and subsequent isolation in, these
islands.

Most of the material has long been known and in
some cases repeatedly described and illustrated, so much
so that repetition seems almost aimless. Many of these
objects are, however, the background on which any
treatise of this nature has to be laid, and nothing else
of equal value exists to substitute for them. Where,
however, it has been possible the illustrations have
been selected from the less familiar or less accessible
pieces.

I have commented above on the want of historical
method in the early part of Romilly Allen's work, and
it may well be that the same accusation will be launched
against myself, inasmuch as it will be seen that in some
instances I have chosen to put on one side the evidence
afforded by associated finds in favour of treatment of
the objects on their own merits. It will be realized that
the problem is seriously complicated by the existence of
these associated finds, if accepted at their face-value.
As is well known, owing to the discovery of remains of
a culture of a Hallstattian complexion, the beginning

of the Iron Age in this country has in recent years been extended backwards to 500 B.C. in order to preserve the previously accepted date of 400 years before the Christian era for the advent of culture of the continental la Tène period and its development in this country. Four and a half centuries down to the Roman conquest is ample time, indeed it is possibly too ample for this development, and it becomes increasingly so, since the investigator will discover that four vessels, each of 100 'years'' burden, have been sent to sea with little or no cargo in their holds, and that he is compelled at the last moment to overload a fifth vessel, a small one of only fifty years' burden, with something like three-quarters of the artistic material for study.

In all ornamental systems a gradual development can be traced, and, though anachronisms are occasionally to be met with, there is always observable a steady process of stylistic evolution which it is not permissible to ignore. No one, for example, would lump together late Gothic, early Tudor, Elizabethan, and Jacobean art in one short period of fifty years, yet that represents fairly closely the process involved in the matter of Celtic ornament, if the apparent validity of certain associated finds is too rigidly insisted upon. Considerations of a quasi-historical nature furnished by such finds must be employed with the greatest caution, unless it can be clearly shown that the character of the objects thus associated is stylistically and chronologically harmonious.

It is an assured conviction that an attempt has been made to stack into the hold a cargo greater than the little vessel I have pictured above is capable of carrying that has led me in the earlier chapters of this little book to distribute some part of it at least to the larger vessel chartered for the preceding voyage. But even this leaves three vessels still with a record of almost empty holds. To one some small quantity of goods can certainly be allotted, but for the other two it becomes a question whether they should ever be regarded as having carried any important quota towards the development of Celtic art in Britain. They are at the best mere transports for those pioneers who constructed the wharves at which the later comers unloaded their cargoes, and who established the depots through which the goods were subsequently distributed over the country. There is, moreover, ample evidence that the national development of Celtic ornament progressed along regional lines, a phenomenon which adds at once to the complexity and fascination of its study. When, therefore, in reconstructing the evolution of the art as a whole it is seen that what is obviously a decadent phase of one regional style occurs side by side with a moderately pure phase of another, the danger of using unreservedly finds which contain examples of a fine expression of the first of these styles in an otherwise late context tends to become intensified, and an element of confusion is thereby introduced. Admittedly the puzzle is no simple one, but its solution becomes no easier if such methods are followed in the endeavour to establish a relative chronology, much less an absolute chronology, of the artistic antiquities of the period. These, in the main, consist of objects in bronze (a few only are of gold) and in a minor degree decorated pottery and wood. The ornamentation of the pottery, an adjunct of everyday domestic life, naturally does not reach a very exalted standard, and thus it is from the metal objects that the principal information on the ornament is to be acquired.

Even these, however, are in many cases clearly *objets de luxe*, as indicated by their scarcity on otherwise prolific habitation-sites, and consequently are such as would be the more likely to be subject to the fickle dictates of changing fashion, even if some allowances be made for relatively more rapid innovations in one district than in another.

In endeavouring to trace the history of Celtic ornament in these islands I have set certain bounds to the scope of my inquiry. In the first place, I have refrained from entering into the maze of discussion in which the problem of the P and Q Celts has been involved, nor do I propose to examine in detail the routes by which the Celts arrived on these shores or the dates at which they first appeared.

Secondly, even though people of Celtic stock may, as already noted, have settled in Britain during the Bronze Age, yet the art of that period is hardly characteristic of what is generally understood in this country by Celtic, and in any case is far from striking, nor does it play any important part in the formation of the phase with which these chapters are concerned. It consists of little more than a system of simple patterns of circles, triangles, chevrons, lozenges, and other linear designs on pottery, goldsmith's work, bronze implements, and other objects. Some slight attempts at novelty, such as ribs terminating in bosses on the face of socketed axes or the clever use of repoussé rings and bosses on bronze shields, are nevertheless of so simple a character as hardly to merit any title to be called art of more than a primitive kind.

Thirdly, I have restricted my inquiry to the period connoted by 'Pagan Times' in the title of Romilly

Allen's work, thus breaking off the history of Celtic art in the early days of the Anglo-Saxon settlements. For while there is no lack of continuity between the earlier period and its successor, and thus the inclusion of some survey of the art of Christian period might reasonably be expected, yet the lines of its development have been more fully studied and its course is more adequately understood. It is the pagan period which has seemed to call for more thorough examination, so as to provide an introduction in itself to the splendours of the amazing revival witnessed by the succeeding 500 years.

I
THE BEGINNINGS

WITH the elimination of the Bronze Age the field of inquiry is at once considerably narrowed; it will be found to embrace a period the beginning of which almost coincides with that of a protohistoric age in Britain, the hour when these islands first appear in history, namely, the date of Pytheas's voyage. It is in fact the age which Sir Augustus Woollaston Franks and others after him have designated by the name of the Late Celtic period. The name is a convenient one, if in some sense misleading. It was intended to connote an age during which the art and culture of these islands not only embraced some manifestations akin to those known from continental material of the centuries immediately preceding the Christian era, but also an extension of that art involving changes and developments to which the rest of Celtic Europe affords no parallels. It covers in fact the later phases of an art which, springing from the Celts of the Continent, was transmitted to Britain, and lived on in these islands for over a thousand years after its life-force had been sapped and practically extinguished elsewhere by the extension of the Roman Empire to Gaul, the Rhine Valley, and the Danube.

The title la Tène IV has been applied to a certain term of this greater period, to cover the interval between the extinction of la Tène III in Gaul and the final conquest of Britain in the first century of our era, but I am doubtful whether Déchelette was happy in his use of this subdivision. As I hope to show, much that he would have included under la Tène IV had in reality passed beyond the stage at which the title is strictly

B

justifiable, into a further stage in which the Celtic
phantasy had already begun to infuse into its art
entirely fresh conceptions, laying the foundations of an
insular character that it was to retain until it died out in
the Middle Ages, after the Norman Conquest in the
eleventh century.

To understand the course of the development of
Celtic art in the narrower sense with which we are here
concerned, it is essential to keep clearly in view the
conditions under which the first seeds were implanted
in British soil. The Bronze Age endured here long after
it had passed away over the greater part of Europe, but
in the centuries preceding its close in Britain new types
of implements appear, brought by an influx into Kent
and the eastern counties of people who, as the distribution of hoards containing similar objects in France goes
to prove, had been forced to evacuate their original
homes in central eastern France. The same causes
which set this first dispersal in motion drove other
immigrants along the same road, but the later comers
for the most part descended on different parts of the
country, and thus it is that the occurrence of the culture
which is typologically, though by no means chronologically, equivalent to the latest stages of the Hallstatt
culture on the Continent has come to light in Sussex,
Wiltshire, and Hampshire in the south, and in Yorkshire
in the north. As we know from finds in southern
England, it remained more or less static, though it pene-
trated some distance into the Midlands, and in a small
degree even to Cambridgeshire, before it was superseded
by fresh influences from abroad. It is interesting to note
the gradual diffusion of new bands of immigrants at
points farther and farther away from the south-east

corner of this island. One example of the evidence on
which this observation is based will suffice. Sussex
with its persistent Hallstatt culture has up to the present
time produced but few examples of the la Tène I
brooch; when we reach Wiltshire, farther west, we find
numerous specimens. At All Cannings Cross they were
actually associated with the pottery of Hallstatt types
which distinguishes that site. Sussex, in fact, represents
an earlier wave of the same movement. Clearly these
late Hallstatt folk on their trek northwards had no time
to change their ceramic style, but could either bring
with them or import after their landing in Britain such
trifles of commerce as new-fashioned fibulae for their
womenkind. Beyond Wiltshire the la Tène I fibula is
found as far west as Cornwall, and northwards into the
Midlands of Gloucestershire, Oxfordshire, and Berkshire, while at the other end it appears in Yorkshire,
where also the pottery is in the main more allied to
continental Hallstatt than to la Tène types.[1] Once
established in this country the pottery had little cause
to change except at points where fresh immigrants
introduced new styles. Thus it comes about, curiously
enough, that with the exception of a small group of
material that found its way into the lower reaches of the
Thames, the first manifestations of anything akin to la
Tène culture appear most markedly on the outer fringe
of the steady flow of immigration which marks the last
two centuries before the landing of Caesar. But the
scarcity of other la Tène types stamps the first Iron Age
immigration as mainly Hallstattian in character.

[1] A fibula of this type from Suffolk (now in the Ashmolean Museum)
differs from the other British examples, and has all the appearance of
an importation from the Continent.

It is indeed from la Tène II that Britain received the bulk of the material with which to lay the foundations of the future system of Late Celtic art; but here, again, we meet with a phenomenon similar to that which marks the earlier stage. Strangely enough, the la Tène II fibula is very rare in this country, while a derivative of la Tène II continental pottery, consisting of pedestalled and cordoned wares which were brought in by immigrants into Britain at various points from Essex to Dorset, is accompanied here not by la Tène II, but, as at Aylesford, by la Tène III fibulae. It is, however, to this possibly initial Belgic wave that the numerous la Tène II swords and daggers found in the Thames and south-east Britain are probably to be assigned.

But with all this constant flow of immigration it becomes difficult to state categorically at what, if any, particular point the first impulse was given to the evolution of the insular phase of Celtic art. All we can say is that the antiquities discovered seem to confirm the existence of at least two well-defined cultural regions, even in so small an area as that part of Britain which is bounded on the west by a line from the head of the Bristol Channel to Yorkshire; and each of these regions seems responsible for some particular contribution towards the shaping of the insular development of Celtic ornament prior to the Roman Conquest.

Before proceeding, however, to examine these more closely, it will be well to clear the ground of those examples that seem to antedate this period of specialization. Some of them indeed may, like the swords, be direct imports from the Continent; it is all the more curious, therefore, that the one piece which more than any has the appearance of being an import should have

been found not in south-eastern England, but in
northern Wales. I refer to the fragmentary bronze
hanging-bowl from Cerrig-y-Drudion, Denbighshire
(fig. 1),[1] the decoration of which retains to the full the

Fig. 1. Bronze hanging-bowl from Cerrig-y-Drudion, Denbighshire.

tradition of the palmette from which the larger element of
Celtic design is ultimately to be derived. Not only does
the decoration of the bowl show close affinities with that
of Armorican vases—possibly an offshoot from the same
parent stock—but it can be traced back to such pieces as
the helmet from Berru, Marne, or to that other bowl from

[1] *Ant. Journ.* vi. 277, figs. 1–2.

Les Saulces-Champenoises, Ardennes.[1] Presumably the bowl from Wales came in at some point far down the

Channel coast, where too must have landed the band of immigrants who were ultimately responsible for the development of one of the schools of design to which I have referred. Strangely enough the bowl bears on itself the hall-mark of that school, and apparently at its very earliest stage, namely, the so-called basketry-decoration. To this group I shall return later.

There are other early examples, some of them constituting a group whose distribution is of special importance, since it serves to indicate the rapidity with which this Celtic art must have spread over a large part of the British Isles. It begins for convenience with the shield-boss from the Thames at Wandsworth, now in the British Museum (fig. 2 a); it is succeeded by another portion of a shield-ornament from the River Witham, Lincolnshire (fig. 2b),[2] and by the shield[3] and sword (fig. 3)[4] from the same river. Then comes what is apparently a minor example

FIG. 3. Bronze scabbard-mount from R. Witham, Lincolnshire.

---

[1] Déchelette, *Manuel*, ii, figs. 655–6.
[2] J. M. Kemble, *Horae Ferales*, 191, pl. XVI.
[3] Ibid., 190, pl. XIV; *British Museum Guide to Early Iron Age Antiquities*, 1925, figs. 114–15. All subsequent references are to this edition.
[4] *Catalogue of Antiquities at Alnwick Castle*, 66, no. 276.

FIG. 2. (a) Bronze shield-boss from R. Thames at Wandsworth. (b) Bronze mount of shield from R. Witham. British
Museum.

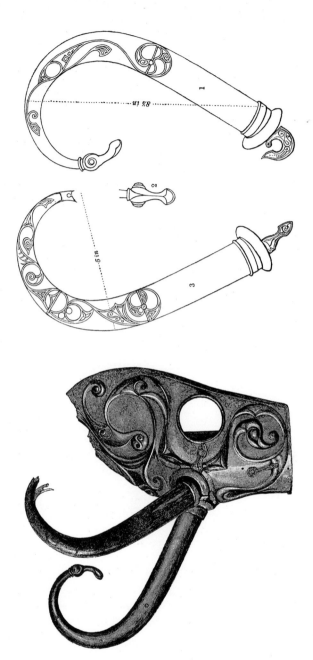

FIG. 4. Bronze champfrein from Torrs, Kirkcudbrightshire.

of the same school, a scabbard-chape from Glencotho
Farm, near Stanhope, Peeblesshire,[1] leading on to one
of the most striking of the early Celtic objects, the
champfrein or head-piece for a horse, from Torrs,
Kirkcudbrightshire,[2] in Galloway (fig. 4), and finally to
the scabbards from the crannog at Lisnacroghera,[3] in
County Antrim, Northern Ireland (fig. 5). I do not mean
to suggest that all of these are imports, but they all bear
the impress of a common style, and indeed some of the
principal pieces echo in so marked a degree the peculiar
treatment of the continental palmette design, that I feel
convinced that they were at least made by Celts who had
broken away from a region where this style was in vogue
at the very hour of their departure, and conserved the
same style up to the time of, and subsequently to, their
landing in Britain. It is not part of my task to trace its
passage across Gaul. It will suffice to cite examples of
the style in question, such as the scabbard from
Cernon-sur-Coole, Dept. Marne (fig. 6).[4]

The features which stamp this particular treatment of
the palmette design are a series of repoussé scrolls,
branching into formal leaves, either open or closed, and
terminating in engraved tendrils with small closely
wound spiral coils and a slender half-closed leaf. In
addition the leaves are often filled with secondary engraved lines following the shape of the leaf itself.[5] A

---

[1] *Proc. Soc. Ant. Scot.* xxxiv. 254, fig. 1.   [2] Ibid. lvi. 21, figs. 2–3.
[3] *B.M. Guide (Iron Age)*, fig. 192; *Journ. R. Hist. and Arch. Ass. of
Ireland* (1883–4), 4th S., vol. vi, figs. on pp. 384, 385, 389, 390.
[4] Déchelette, *Manuel*, ii, fig. 463, 2–2a; fig. 480.
[5] A scabbard, now in Hull Museum, from the R. Trent (recorded
and figured in *Yorks. Arch. Journal*, xxxi. 94), exhibits an interesting
development of this feature. Details of the scabbard's shape in themselves speak of a later time, and so too do the unintelligent and futile
circlets that fill up the leaflets without any regard for their form or line.

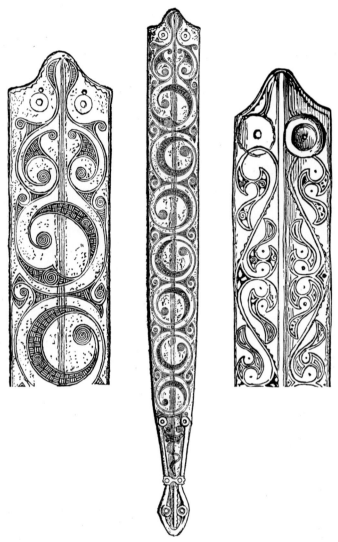

Fig. 5. Bronze scabbards from Lisnacroghera, Co. Antrim, N. Ireland.

C

further feature is the termination of some of the scrolls
in a round or oval motive, enclosing a central spot, to
which is added a beak-like finial, producing the effect of
a bird's head at the end of a long winding stalk. Whether
the motive was originally con-
ceived as ornithomorphic I am
not prepared to say; but certainly
on the Cernon-sur-Coole scabbard, as on the Wandsworth
shield-boss and on other British
pieces, it seems to have been carried to a point where its bird-like
character appears absolutely in-
tentional. Apart from the strongly
embossed relief of the scrolls and
other portions of the design, seldom found in England outside
the group, we again note on the
Wandsworth boss the presence of
engraved motives within some of
the panels formed by the embossed work. These present the
same closely wound spirals and
the same slender terminal leaves.
It is also true of the shield and

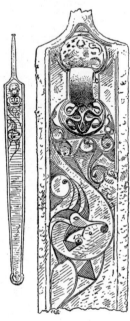

FIG. 6. Sword and detail
of bronze scabbard from
Cernon-sur-Coole, Dept.
Marne, France.

scabbard from the Witham, for though here the bird's
head is not in evidence, the engraved spirals serve
to place them beyond dispute in the same class. The
Glencotho Farm chape shows a rather poor version
of the bird's head motive; this, however, with all the
other concomitants of the style are in full evidence on
the Torrs champfrein. Not only does the bird's head
appear in relief at the end of one of the scrolls on the

frontlet, but is also engraved on the horns, and finally occurs in the round at their tips. It has in addition one small detail, which, so far as I am aware, hardly occurs again in exactly this form until Christian times—a fragment of key-pattern employed to fill up a panel of engraving on one of the horns.

By an easy crossing from Galloway the style was transported to the shores of Ulster, and so we find that the Lisnacroghera scabbards share not only the same spiral coils, but also the practice of filling the leaves with internal lines or motives adjusted to the outline of the leaf itself. A further common trait appears on one scabbard, where the edges of the scrolls are decorated with an indented border, in a manner frequently observable on objects belonging to the continental school with which the whole of this British group is associated. But Lisnacroghera is the outermost representative of the school; and consequently we need not be surprised if, as we shall see later, it also absorbed another element of design derived, in my opinion, from one of the two native schools to which I have already alluded.

The Witham shield includes among its ornamental motives a good example of the base of the palmette. This gives us our first clue towards placing what has been regarded as the finest example of Celtic work in Britain, the famous Battersea shield.[1] Here the decoration is in a lighter and more tenuous style; it is, however, to be noted that the quasi-triangular panels at the base of the enclosed palmettes in the central disk are filled with coils ending in the same leaflets as appear in the decoration of the large Wandsworth-Witham group.

[1] B.M. Guide (Iron Age), 106, pl. 1.

It may be asked whether any special line of immigration can be detected to which so wide a diffusion of this
specialized group might be attributed. Clearly it would
seem to have been borne northwards by settlers endeavouring to effect a foothold at some point along the
east coast, and travelling northwards, in that endeavour,
past the Wash to Lincolnshire and beyond. Without
venturing to designate them by any specific name—for
the attachment of the classical names to any particular
body of immigrants is parlous work—it may be assumed
on archaeological grounds that they were not unconnected with the chariot-burial folk of the East Riding
of Yorkshire. As we have seen, the special traits of the
group of objects passed under review exhibit close
affinities with a style that finds its counterparts from
Switzerland to the Marne region, a style that may be
accredited to the continental la Tène II period. I am
authoritatively informed that this phase of decoration is
rather poorly represented in France itself, as though its
parents had carried it elsewhere shortly after its birth.
Without insisting rigidly on the conclusions which it
might be possible to draw from British material in this
connexion, it is noteworthy that a very large series of
scabbards of the form assigned to la Tène II by continental archaeologists has been found not only in the
Thames but elsewhere in this country. We have every
warrant for believing that it was the la Tène II period, and
a fairly early phase of it at that, which witnessed one of
the larger influxes of Celtic immigrants into this country.
The Thames scabbards fall into line with the Wandsworth shield and the Thames boss; the Witham specimen goes hand in hand with the shield from that river.

It is not of course hereby implied that all la Tène II

scabbards are connected with this particular movement. They may belong to several stages of immigration initiated during this cultural period. It is merely suggested that evidence exists of immigration by a particular body that ultimately concentrated its attempts rather towards the north. Many of the la Tène II swords are doubtless connected with an immigration of a far more important character, and somewhat later in date, in a more southerly area.

On the Yorkshire Wolds we meet with associations of a similar character to those from Lincolnshire and farther south. The chariot-burial at Grimthorpe affords an excellent illustration.[1] The sword and scabbard are of la Tène II type. The decoration with studs of red enamel is in the earliest form in which the technique appears in this country; it is repeated on the disks associated with the Bugthorpe sword.[2] Even the shell-like ornament on the chape of the Grimthorpe scabbard can be paralleled on the Witham shield,[3] where its origin in a group of petals detached from a complete palmette can be clearly recognized, though the process of stylization which led to its transformation into a scallop is already in evidence. The same scallop motive appears on a Hunsbury scabbard,[4] but, as in the case of that from Bugthorpe, along with another form of decoration which has a somewhat later history (see p. 21).

The Grimthorpe sword, however, seems to stand in an earlier line, a supposition that gains corroboration from the remarkable shield found in the same grave. The decoration as a whole is unlike anything found

---

[1] J. R. Mortimer, *Forty Years*, 150, frontispiece; *Reliquary*, ix. 180.
[2] *B.M. Guide (Iron Age)*, 114, figs. 124–5.
[3] Ibid. fig. 115.
[4] *Ass. Arch. Soc. Reports*, xviii. 58, pl. III, 2.

elsewhere in this country, save perhaps that the curious quadripartite oval design at the centre recurs on one or two minor pieces. The border, on the other hand, is possibly unique, and would seem to have had its origin in the key-pattern, which reappears on the Torrs champfrein, on wood from Glastonbury,[1] and on ferrules of spears at Lisnacroghera.[2] Parallels to details of the decoration of this specialized group under review have already been cited from la Tène itself, and it is there too that we find an extraordinarily close counterpart to the unusual treatment of the key-pattern on a scabbard from the same site.[3] Though not by any means so close, the detail and general character of the decoration on the scabbard-mouth and ferrules from Lisnacroghera[4] have much in them that recalls the ornamentation of another scabbard from la Tène.[5]

The chain of evidence for the diffusion of objects forming, so far as these islands are concerned, a restricted but homogeneous group, would seem to indicate that the arrival of Celtic culture in Ireland during the early Iron Age was by way of the Tyne gap and the Solway Firth. A glance at the considerations, supported by a large series of maps, presented by Dr. Cyril Fox in his admirable essay on *The Personality of Britain* demonstrates that throughout early archaeological time the Palaeozoic zone in England acted as a barrier to communication between Great Britain and Ireland, at

[1] A. Bulleid, and H. St. G. Gray, *Glastonbury*, pl. L, XI.

[2] *Journ. R. Hist. and Arch. Ass. of Ireland* (1883–4), 4th S., vol. vi, fig. on p. 394.

[3] P. Vouga, *La Tène*, fig. 7 n.

[4] *Journ. R. Hist. and Arch. Ass. of Ireland* (1883–4), 4th S., vol. vi, p. 391, and p. 394 lower fig.

[5] P. Vouga, *La Tène*, fig. 7 j.

any rate in the diffusion of culture from one to the other. Such only passed through one or two breaches in that barrier; and of these Dr. Fox discounts that which leads across the Midlands to Cheshire as of little importance compared with the more northerly route through the Tyne valley. As the maps show, there is to be found in Ireland a group of archaeological material corresponding to the line of finds of different periods distributed along that route. Not the whole of Ireland is affected thereby, but just that portion of it, the north-east quarter roughly comprising Ulster and northern Leinster. When the analogous objects on both sides of the Irish Channel are compared, both quantitatively and typologically the Irish group will be found to lag behind.[1] There are vast stores of archaeological material from the Bronze Age; there are great riches of artistic products from the seventh century onwards, but for the interval of some 800 years the showing is meagre in the extreme.

[1] My Irish friends may detect some political bias in the views I have propounded. There is none. I have long been an advocate of the Atlantic sea-route in archaeology, but, in spite of intensive search, I am unable to detect any trace of sea-borne importation of Celtic art belonging to the early Iron Age to Ireland other than across the narrows of the Irish Channel. Ireland is disappointingly poor in material comparable to that which illustrates the early period of Celtic art in Britain.

II

THE BRITISH DEVELOPMENT

THE next stage in the development of Celtic art in Britain is best explained by words used in 1897 by Sir Arthur Evans in describing a deposit of gold objects found on the north-east coast of Ireland.[1] He says: 'The tendency of all Late-Celtic art was to reduce the naturalistic motives borrowed by it from the classical world to geometrical schemes.' And, inasmuch as the art survived longer in Britain than on the Continent, it follows that we find that this process of reduction from the natural to the geometric carried to a point far beyond any reached on the mainland.

We have seen that even in the early part of the immigrations there were still numerous objects on which the origins of Celtic ornament are clearly discernible. But, when the process mentioned above had once set in, its effect was so rapid that within quite a short while little trace of the palmette or other original constituent motives is to be detected.

The whole character of the art has changed. The Celts have broken free from the trammels of a borrowed style and have created for themselves one of their own, in which everything is expressed in curving lines, arranged in designs often of amazing intricacy. Balance and symmetry vie with daring and ingenuity in producing a decoration at once satisfying and at its best free from a certain measure of restlessness and misunderstanding which marks its last efforts to preserve the traditions of the continental style which gave it birth.

What is interesting in all this is that, in spite of the

[1] *Archaeologia*, lv. 404.

unrest in Gaul due to the advance of Rome, and possibly because that advance stopped the natural channels of artistic movement, the Celts in Britain succeeded in developing what may truly be termed a national style. Indeed, the mere fact that they were spared from more than a momentary invasion for a hundred years after Caesar's conquest of Gaul gave them just the necessary breathing-space to bring this style to full birth; and it was their ultimate fortune that the British Isles never came wholly under Roman domination, so that there always remained a corner where the native art could survive even if in a greatly weakened condition. When in full time freedom is regained, it will appear, as it were, in a state of convalescence after a long and wasting illness. Indeed, the wonder is that the patient should have recovered at all. The subsequent art-history of these islands during the seventh to tenth centuries proves that the recovery not only took place, but that it resulted in a fresh access of vigour, leading eventually to some of the greatest masterpieces of that age.

Unfortunately, as already stated, it is still impossible to determine exactly in which particular area of Britain were generated the first impulses towards the creation of this national style. Up to the present time our knowledge of the earliest part of the Iron Age in Britain is limited to discoveries on sites that have produced little of great artistic merit. The pottery of the so-called Hallstatt style is far from being distinguished in character, and even the early la Tène classes are not such as to suggest more than that the Celts had brought with them that sense of line which is the key-note of their later continental art. The chance discoveries already mentioned prove that the art was there, but we still await the opening of some site which shall produce a large series of objects affording us a conspectus of the development of the art through all its stages down to Roman times.

In saying this, it is no intention of mine to belittle the exploratory work of the past or even of the present time. All I wish to convey is that the vast mass of evidence of intense activity on the part of the Celts, afforded, for example, by the network of hill-fortresses, some of stupendous size, scattered over large parts of Britain, particularly in the south and west, which cannot all have been raised in a day, nor even in a brief space of years, gives reason to hope that in due course some of them, or an adjacent site, will yield up the material upon which the surer foundations of any survey of this early Celtic ornament in Britain can be well and truly laid.

At the moment our evidence is of three kinds:

(1) From graves; e.g. Yorkshire barrows, at Arras, Kilham, and other sites;[1] Birdlip, Gloucestershire;[2] Stamford Hill, Plymouth,[3] Devon; Harlyn Bay, Cornwall,[4] and the like—a few scattered examples of burial by inhumation and of widely different dates. Cremation-graves of the first century B.C. in the eastern counties are more numerous, but are with a few exceptions not particularly rich, while of later burials, e.g. Welwyn[5] and Stanfordbury,[6] some are rich, but not very informative, and all are in any case too late to speak of Celtic ornament at its earlier stages.

(2) From hoards; e.g. Santon Downham[7] and West-

---

[1] *Archaeologia*, lx. 251 ff.
[2] Ibid. lxi. 331.　　　　　　　　　　　[3] Ibid. xl. 500.
[4] *Ant. Journ.* i. 283.
[5] *Archaeologia*, lxiii, 1.
[6] Ibid. p. 9; C. Fox, *Archaeology of the Cambridge Region*, 99.
[7] *Cambs. Ant. Soc. Proc. and Comm.* xiii. 146.

hall,[1] Suffolk; Saham Toney,[2] Norfolk; Stanwick,[3] Yorkshire; Polden Hill,[4] Somersetshire; and Seven Sisters,[5] Glamorgan. These do allow of some conception of the nature of the products contained in the hoard up to the time of deposition, but unfortunately the evidence in most cases points definitely to a comparatively late date for their deposition—that is, in the first century after Christ, some just before, others after the Roman Conquest, and we are still unable to be certain that all the constituents of the hoard are contemporary. Even if some are older, they nevertheless fall considerably below the period at which I have ventured to set the special (possibly imported) group described above.

(3) From habitation-sites. Here full justice must be done to the long and untiring zeal with which year after year the explorers add to our knowledge by their excavations at Meare and Glastonbury. To them we owe the only possibility we possess at the present time of drawing anything like a complete picture of the life, habits, and material culture of a group of people during a century or more before the coming of Caesar.

With all that we are bound to admit that two communities living in sites of a nature closely akin to that of the Irish crannogs can hardly be considered as representing the apogee of the civilization to which they belonged. Rather do they give the impression of refugees seeking, as did the Saxons of the Fenlands round the Wash at the time of the Norman Conquest,

---

[1] *Archaeologia*, xxxvi. 454.
[2] *V.C.H., Norfolk*, i. 273 and plate.
[3] *Proc. Arch. Inst.*, 1846 (York), 34–8; *B.M. Guide (Iron Age)*, 138; *Archaeologia*, lx. 288; *Catalogue of Antiquities at Alnwick Castle*, 88.
[4] *Archaeologia*, xiv. 90.
[5] *Arch. Cambrensis*, 1905, pp. 127 ff.

an asylum in inaccessible fens, driven by *force majeure* to leave their strongholds on the highlands of Wiltshire, Somerset, and Dorset. In any case the period covered by the lake-dwellings of Somerset hardly extends far behind the beginning of the first century B.C., so that such art as the relics recovered from these sites display must have already behind it a considerable history since the time it was first brought into this island.

We are nevertheless fortunate in possessing a few objects that serve to illustrate this past history; and these

FIG. 7. Details of gold torc from Clevedon, Somerset.

fall into line with what we know from farther east. Mention has already been made of the hanging-bowl from Denbighshire, found, it is true, well away from the main area of the western cultural group, but from the very place of its discovery hardly to be ascribed to any other agents for its transmission to North Wales. Another important piece is the beautiful, though fragmentary, gold torc from Clevedon, Somerset,[1] now in the British Museum (fig. 7). It has palmettes executed in a manner characteristic of a fine period of Celtic art. It has a further importance, in that these designs are accompanied by a method of decoration which subsequently occupies a strong position in the ornament of

[1] *B.M. Guide (Iron Age)*, 150, fig. 175.

the western group. This consists of filling in the background with lines arranged in small groups, alternatively vertical and horizontal, producing the effect of basketry. This method of decoration is in its essence one common to pottery of many epochs; it is also employed, as Mr. Reginald Smith has pointed out, on metal-work of the Hallstatt period on the Continent.[1] Something similar also appears on the Denbighshire bowl. But on all these earlier examples it merely amounts to a system of hatching in alternating groups, usually triangles, sometimes even with curving lines to accommodate it to the shape of a vase or other object of rounded form. It is never used to cover large surfaces, nor, as in the British style, is it executed in such small groups of short lines. On the best examples it leaps to the eye as conscious imitation of basketry or chequered weaving. A certain lack of regularity in the groups of lines enhances the effect. Later it tends to become more regular, more studied, and thereby loses much of the charm which its earlier manner of execution lends to the object that it serves to adorn.

This is proved by the fact that the patterns, to which it forms the background, also fall away from the standard of purity of curving lines which the earlier pieces strive to preserve. In short, the decline in its appearance goes hand in hand with the geometrical character that stamps the development of Celtic ornament from about 50 B.C. onwards.

The process of geometrization must have set in with considerable rapidity as soon as the Celtic immigrants had settled down in their new homes, since we rarely find any decorated objects that at once recall the source

[1] *Ant. Journ.* vi. 277–8.

from which Celtic art derived its original inspiration. For it is hard to believe that, had the art in its earlier state survived for ever so short a time, more examples of its use would not have come down to us. As it is, the ornamented material by which we are able to gauge the trend of decorative fashion during the centuries before the Roman Conquest is so predominantly geometric in character, that, comparatively late though most of it appears to be, the change must almost be said to have been initiated from the very first years of the settlement.

Without a knowledge of their ancestry it would be difficult to detect, at first glance, in the patterns employed on the pottery from Meare and Glastonbury the source to which the already formalized scrolls on the la Tène II pottery of the Marne region still bear witness. The leaf designs and certain scrolled patterns have advanced so far on the road of stylization that their relationship to continental ornament has wellnigh lost all reality. It is rather such elements as the key-pattern, as it appears at Glastonbury, that take us straight back to the Continent.

Let it suffice to say that little of our material evidence for a study of Celtic design can be dated before the first century B.C., and by that time the flight from the natural to the geometric had been practically completed. The older designs were tending to lose their meaning; and imitation was reducing them to so poor a shadow of their former beauty that the flight to which I have alluded is, in its essence, a fresh effort on the part of the British Celts, now far removed from the classical world from which the first inspiration was drawn, to replace something that had become unintelligible and unreal by a new system of ornament capable of satisfying their

aesthetic needs and their appreciation of the value of
curving line as a basis of decoration—an art in which at
their best they had few rivals.

Among the material available for the study of this
art-period there are certain objects—isolated finds, but
pieces of obvious importance—which at first sight do
not appear to fall easily into line with the most marked
tendencies of their time, and thus pre-
sent difficulties in any attempt to assign
them to their proper position in the
scheme of Celtic artistic products. The
outstanding example that comes to mind
is the Battersea shield. I have already
remarked on one minor feature of its
decoration that gives it some claim to
be placed at a relatively early date.

There are, however, others that speak
in the same sense. The enclosed palmette in itself is a good sign-post. It is
executed in a manner, in my opinion,
quite impossible after the first century

FIG. 8. Detail of
ornament on bronze
fibula of la Tène I
form from Huns-
bury, Northants.

B.C., and, I should strongly suspect, improbable after
the end of the second. It falls thus into line with
other known examples of the use of this motive, as on
the Clevedon torc, and, if a date is needed, it is
furnished by the decoration on the bow of one of the
fibulae of la Tène I form from Hunsbury, Northamptonshire (fig. 8). As Mr. Reginald Smith has
recorded,[1] the decoration consists of a band of palmettes, but these can only be imperfectly realized in
his illustration. The appended figure, in which the

---

[1] *Archaeological Journal*, lxix, p. 427, fig. 3; figure reproduced in
Arch. Cambrensis, 1927, p. 83, fig. 16.

pattern is developed, will give a more accurate idea of its delicacy and its clever adaptation of the palmette for the purpose. Its occurrence on a la Tène I fibula (which, however, I would hardly dare to place so far back in this country as Mr. Smith has suggested) supported as it is by its discovery at Hunsbury, does distinctly argue for a relatively early dating for this use of the design in so pure a form.

Secondly, the enamel comes into question. It has admittedly been questioned whether enamel in elaborate cloison-like cells set in key-pattern can be early at all, but the very nature of the cells should warn us that the work is not late, for key-pattern is distinctly rare, except in early work. Moreover, the bulk of Celtic enamel in this country, known to belong to the pre-Roman period, is executed in champlevé technique, and this technique remains in vogue down to the end of the period under review in this book. Once the technique had developed, it was used to the exclusion of almost all others. Previously the methods of securing enamel to the object which it was intended to decorate take a variety of forms. Initially, and most commonly, as so often remarked, it appears as conical or hemispherical studs, secured through the centre by a bronze rivet, e.g. the Bugthorpe disk, and these were intended to replace the use of coral for the same purpose. Another method of constructing bosses was to score the surface of the bronze with cross-hatchings, as on the Thames helmet,[1] in order to hold the enamel from shifting laterally; but even so a central rivet was required, and the brittle substance was, as in the case of the conical studs, still exposed to the danger of any blow. The con-

[1] *B.M. Guide* (*Iron Age*), p. 107, fig. 116.

struction of the bosses on the Battersea shield is perhaps an attempt to surmount the difficulty—a difficulty that was entirely removed when the champlevé process allowed the artificer to sink large spots below the surface-plane of the metal, or, by cutting away the metal, to fill up the design from behind, the enamel being keyed in place by the undercutting of the metal. The Battersea studs are one of those ingenious attempts to overcome a problem that all ages have produced, but, even if no other reasons existed, the use of the key-pattern to form the cells would in itself argue against an advanced date. But, further, the general design—apart from the enclosed palmette, the peculiarly tenuous style of the scrolls, and particularly the manner in which three of the scrolls are brought together at a solid triangle with a spot at its middle, instead of, as one might expect, in an open triangle—is one which is to be encountered commonly and almost exclusively in the second and first centuries B.C. It is a commonplace, for example, of Glastonbury decoration, e.g. the wooden tub and examples of the pottery. It is admirably illustrated by the Yarnton sherd[1] of the decorated Glastonbury variety and in metal on a little boss from Wood Eaton, Oxfordshire (fig. 21 a), a site which has undoubtedly produced many Roman objects, but at the same time la Tène I brooches and other Celtic objects. Since the same treatment of intersecting curves occurs on the Hunsbury scabbard, once more the evidence throws the date of the shield farther back than that which Mr. Hawkes has recently suggested for it.[2]

[1] B.M. Guide (Iron Age), 154, fig. 183.
[2] T. D. Kendrick and C. F. C. Hawkes, Archaeology in England and Wales, 1914–31, p. 205. In short, it adds yet another link with the repertory of la Tène II style (cp. P. Vouga, La Tène, fig. 7 k) from which, as already indicated, Celtic ornament in Britain is so largely derived.

Another object which calls for a similar analysis of its ornament in order to arrive at its stylistic position is the well-known horned helmet from the Thames.[1] It would be difficult to conceive anything more dissimilar in treatment to that of the Battersea shield than the decoration of this interesting piece. If the embossed curves of the shield are to be described as tenuous, those of the helmet are doubly so. They almost defy interpretation in the sense of pattern. The fine, slight lines wander up the surface of the head-piece in a manner in which one seems to picture the craftsman expressing a wayward fancy in a series of curves breaking out into inconspicuous enlargements at indefinite intervals, all seemingly devoid of any relation to any known system of decoration. If indeed they have any meaning at all, their origin might reasonably be sought in a faint remembrance of the tendrils of the palmette, so faint, however, as to incline one to date the helmet rather late. This would, I believe, be to estimate it incorrectly. How then are we to reach a true idea of its position in the repertory of Celtic ornament? Fortunately there are several criteria by which its place can be determined. The first lies in the above-mentioned ornament itself. This is closely comparable with the decoration on the boss of the broken branch still attached to the ring of a bridle-bit from Ulceby, Lincolnshire.[2] This bit, as I shall endeavour to show later, belongs to the earliest class of bridle-bits known from the British Iron Age, the class to which that from Hagbourne Hill, Berkshire,

[1] *B.M. Guide (Iron Age)*, 107, fig. 116.
[2] Now in the Mayer Collection, Liverpool Museum (*Journal Brit. Arch. Ass.* xv. 225, pl. 22, fig. 2); the electrum torcs from the same find (*ibid.* pl. 20, fig. 1 and pl. 21) are in the Evans Collection in the Ashmolean Museum.

Fig. 9. Bronze engraved mirror from Birdlip, Gloucestershire. Gloucester Museum.

also belongs, and which was the forerunner of the specialized series of Irish bits, on some examples of which similar ornamentation occurs. One feature of the Ulceby piece is the pair of studs, in themselves a characteristic of this whole class of bits, set, one on each side of the branch, for the purpose of preventing lateral movement of the ring in the perforation of the branch. The studs on the Ulceby ring take the form of flattish disks decorated with a ring of small bosses enclosing a larger boss at the centre. A terret, probably from Suffolk, formerly in the Fenton Collection, and now in the British Museum, has three such disks along each face of the ring, cast in the solid with the terret itself, and in addition a row of small knobs along its fore-edge. These latter appear to result from a modification of the early knobbed terret as known again from Hagbourne Hill, the type from which the lipped terret of western England subsequently was developed. The variant of the Fenton Collection type seems to belong rather to the eastern counties; its date is established by discovery of the type at Hunsbury, an example having been recently added to the collections in Northampton Museum from that site.

It is these knobs which in an enlarged form appear along the crest of the head-piece and along the sides of the horns of the Thames helmet. Finally, among the scrolled ornament there are not only cross-scored disks to which flat enamel disks were originally riveted, but also small fields decorated with faint basketry ornament, such as is employed in an engraved technique on the Hunsbury scabbard and many of the bronze mirrors. In short, everything points to the helmet belonging to a period antecedent to the replacement of the Hallstatt culture—or rather its British version—of south-west England (Wiltshire, Dorset, Somerset, &c.) by the extension of the Aylesford-Swarling culture of the latter part of the first century B.C. to Northamptonshire, as evidenced by the Duston settlement at no distance from Hunsbury itself, but lower down in the valley instead of on the ridge of the hill south of the town.

I have hinted above at the existence of two schools at this period. Such, it seems, there must have been, since curiously it is only in south-western Britain and certain other areas in direct communication with it (e.g. in Sussex) that pottery decorated with other than the simplest patterns—triangles, groups of spots, and occasionally simple curvilinear designs—are known. The knowledge of this predilection for scrolled decoration even on pottery allows us to assume that some of the finest efforts of this geometric phase must have emanated from the west of Britain.

These are of course best exemplified by the well-known mirrors with engraved backs, which have been found almost exclusively in southern England. Almost all have been described in detail by Mr. Reginald Smith[1], and an additional specimen found at Nijmegen, Holland—a piece which on all counts can claim to be of British workmanship—has recently been published by Mr. G. C. Dunning.[2]

The two finest, those from Birdlip, Gloucestershire (fig. 9), and Desborough, Northamptonshire,[3] are masterpieces of engraved geometric design, and in addition have handles of looped form on which, more particularly in

[1] *Archaeologia*, lxi, 329 ff.
[2] *Journal of the Archaeological Institute*, lxxxv. 69, fig. 1.
[3] *Archaeologia*, lxi, pls. XLII and XLIII.

Fig. 10. Grave-group with cordoned pottery, bronze mirror, and cup from Colchester, Essex. Colchester Museum.

the case of that from Desborough, the Celtic artists have realized to the full their capacity for the invention of graceful mouldings.

The Birdlip mirror, it is true, was found in a grave which also contained a beautiful fibula, regarded as an adaptation of the continental 'Augenfibel', dated by Almgren to *c.* A.D. 40–60. But, in spite of this apparent evidence to the contrary, it is probable that both it and the Desborough mirror should be placed considerably earlier. As Mr. R. G. Collingwood has justly observed in another connexion: 'In the development of any type (and we might here add of any ornament) once established, decadence is the general law of art; and where one meets with an intensely vigorous work, so far removed from the weariness and formalism of a decadent school, it can hardly be a late example of its kind. When the history of a school is drawing to its close, the artist either dully repeats, without conviction and without fervour, patterns which have become mechanical; or else he feels uneasily that this is what he is about to do, and searches for something sensational to relieve the tedium that threatens to engulf him.'[1] We are thus justified in regarding these two mirrors not as the culmination of the phase of artistic production to which they belong, but rather as representatives of that phase's initial efforts, before it fell away from its first high standard of achievement into less careful and less intelligent work. That this is so is to be proved by the numerous examples still preserved to us, on which the workmanship is distinctly poor, marking a gradual decadence in this class of decoration.

Fortunately we possess corroborative evidence for the

[1] Ibid., lxxx. 40.

correctness of this assumption in the present connexion. In the Colchester Museum is a grave-group from Colchester itself (fig. 10) which includes a mirror, un-engraved but with a looped handle, that is stylistically closely allied to those of the Desborough and Birdlip mirrors, but is stiffer and more sophisticated in concep-tion, and is evidently an imitation of the easier work on the other two. With this mirror were associated a neat bronze cup, with handle moulded in accordance with Celtic taste, and also a series of cordoned vases that can now be dated to the latter half of the first century B.C. The Birdlip and Desborough mirrors must therefore be placed before the middle of the century. Next in point of style comes the mirror from Nijmegen, Holland (fig. 11); its handle is a crude imitation of that of the Birdlip mirror, and the engraved design is similarly an unintelligent attempt to reproduce the splendidly balanced patterns of the older examples. On it we note a tendency to reduce the decoration to a series of unconnected circles, each filled with a motive formed of a pair of lentoids arranged side by side in a kind of s-shaped motive, one which recurs with the greatest frequency throughout this phase of Celtic ornament. The same holds good of another small detail; a motive composed of a circle with a smaller circle disposed eccentrically within it, the space between them being filled with hatching. This begins as an open terminal of a scroll, but in due course closes up, and finally, like some amoeba, detaches itself from the main body of the design and floats about in space.

It is in a system of circles with these concomitant details that the decoration is executed in an aimless manner on a mirror from Stamford Hill, near Plymouth,

0   1   2   3   4 in.

G.C.D. 1928.

Fig. 11. Bronze engraved mirror from Nijmegen, Holland.

Devon (fig. 12).[1] To it certainly belongs the stiff moulded handle figured on the same plate, interesting because from the same cemetery came part of another mirror with a handle which, though of Y-form, such as is employed on most of the later mirrors, nevertheless has two good trumpet mouldings at the top, recalling those on the Desborough mirror.[2] The circular treatment of the decoration appears again in the west of England on the mirror from Trelan Bahow, Cornwall (fig. 18),[3] along with a simple Y-handle; but this mirror has an additional point of interest to which I shall have occasion to return later.

Before turning to examine the rest of the mirrors, it may be well to make it clear that it is the Celts of western England that we must credit with the evolution of these magnificently conceived, flamboyant patterns with their basketry filling. In support of this it may be noted that it is used to the best advantage on scabbards with chapes of la Tène II from Meare, Somerset,[4] Hunsbury, Northants. (fig. 13),[5] and Bugthorpe, Yorkshire,[6] and finally on a scabbard of somewhat more advanced type from Amerden, Buckinghamshire,[7] not far from Taplow on the Thames, but in an uninspired manner, as is the case with the interesting spear with applied bronze plate from the Thames.[8] Geographically speaking, Hunsbury and Bugthorpe may seem too far

[1] *Archaeologia*, xl, pl. xxx, fig. 1.
[2] Ibid. figs. 2 and 4.
[3] *B.M. Guide (Iron Age)*, 121, fig. 132.
[4] *Ant. Journ.* x. 154.
[5] *Ass. Arch. Soc. Reports*, xviii. 58, pl. iii. 3; *V. C. H., Northants.* I. pl. opp. p. 147.
[6] *B.M. Guide (Iron Age)*, 114, fig. 124.
[7] *V. C. H., Bucks.* i. 186, fig.
[8] *Man*, 1931, p. 112.

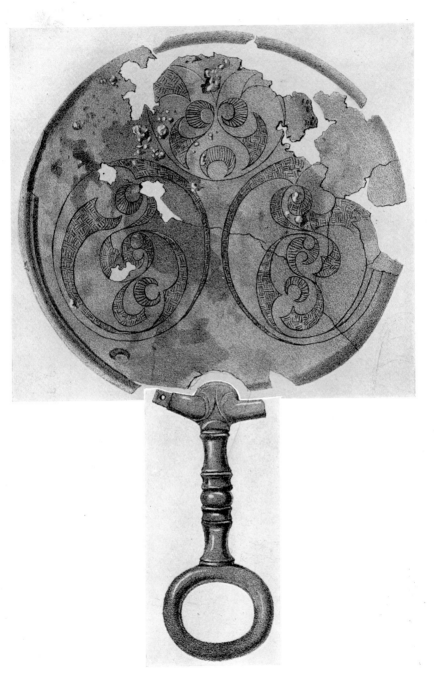

FIG. 12. Bronze engraved mirror from Stamford Hill,
Plymouth. Plymouth Museum.

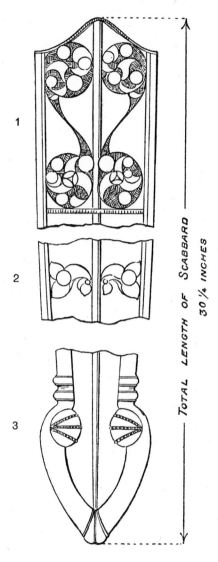

FIG. 13. Details of bronze scabbard
from Hunsbury, Northants.

F

removed from the west of England to have much connexion with it; but in actual practice there were,
particularly towards the end of the second century B.C.,
happenings which tended to bring them politically
together. Even culturally, Northamptonshire down to
the middle of the first century B.C. already belonged, or
was closely allied, to the western group, as its pottery
with decoration of graceful curving lines terminating in
rosettes or spots serves to demonstrate.[1] In any case
these places are connected by the line of the Jurassic
ridge which, it is recognized, constituted an important
factor in early British communication. A lead between
Northamptonshire and Yorkshire is supplied by the
employment of the basketry ornamental technique on
an imperfect bit from Ulceby, north Lincolnshire.[2] It
must be also from this western source that it ultimately
found its way to south-west Scotland and Northern
Ireland. In the first-mentioned area it appears in conjunction with excellent scroll-work and the curled
terminals described above on some curved bronze plates
(possibly parts of a gorget and another long band) at
Balmaclellan, Dumfriesshire,[3] and in the latter on
the sword-scabbards from Lisnacroghera. It is a loan
in each case; for the Balmaclellan examples of this
work were associated with a mirror which can hardly
be much earlier than the first century A.D., and the
Lisnacroghera scabbards have one and all a type of chape
which appears to be peculiar to Ireland, as evidenced
by examples in the British Museum and the National
Museum in Dublin, all of which come from Irish

[1] Hunsbury and Desborough; J. R. Allen, *Celtic Art*, 125, pl. opp.
p. 122; T. J. George, *Hunsbury*, pl. 3.
[2] *Journal Brit. Arch. Ass.* xv. 227, pl. 22, fig. 1.
[3] J. Anderson, *Scotland in Pagan Times (Iron Age)*, 128, fig. 105.

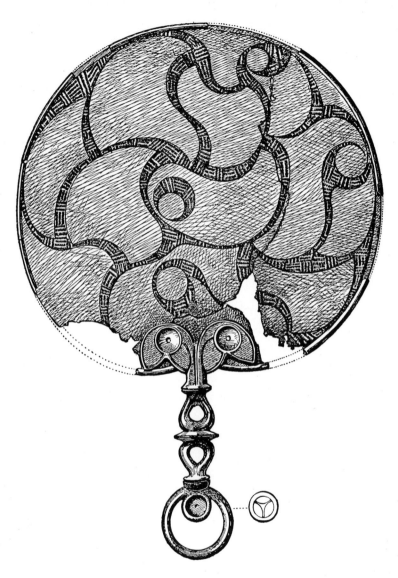

FIG. 14. Bronze engraved mirror from Old Warden, Beds.

localities.[1] On this and other grounds investigated
above, we must conclude that the Irish group is an
offshoot from the Yorkshire culture subsequent to its
adoption of the basketry technique.

It is the very geographical distribution of what are
manifestly inferior productions of this school of ornament which seems to confirm the accuracy of its ascrip-
tion to a western province. When we turn to mirrors
like those from Old Warden, Bedfordshire (fig. 14),[2] from
Rivenhall[3] and Billericay, Essex (fig. 15 a),[4] and others
without provenance in the British Museum,[5] one of
which at least probably comes from Kent, as may
also the example in the Mayer Collection at Liverpool (fig. 15 b),[6] we see at once how far they have fallen
from the high estate of the brilliant western creations.
The design on the Old Warden mirror resembles
nothing so much as a bad jig-saw puzzle, while
its handle is a stiff formal thing, a shade worse
than that on the mirror from the Colchester grave-
group. The remainder all have the ɤ-shaped handle,
either plain or with slight modifications, not always
of a pleasing nature, as on that from Billericay,
which otherwise has a bold but clumsy tripartite
design. This mirror stands close in time to that in
the Mayer Collection, on which the decoration is
arranged in three circles in a manner reminiscent of the
Stamford Hill example. Both, however, have in common
a feature which, as we shall see later, constitutes the hall-
mark of a period of change in the execution of these

---

[1] e.g. Athenry, Co. Galway (J. M. Kemble, *Horae Ferales*, 192, pl.
XVII. 4).

[2] *Archaeologia*, lxi. 333, fig. 3.   [3] Ibid. 337, fig. 5.

[4] Ibid. 337.   [5] Ibid. 340, figs. 7–8.

[6] Its provenance is stated to be the River Thames (ibid. 341).

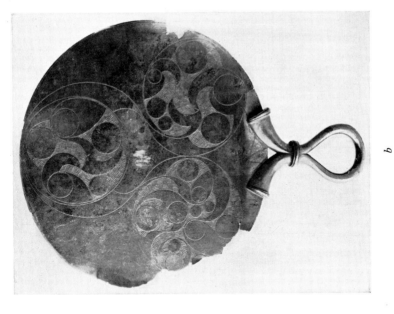

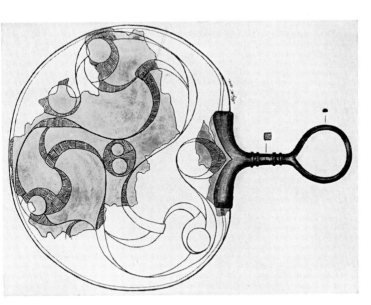

b

a

Fig. 15. Bronze engraved mirrors. (*a*) Billericay, Essex. (*b*) Mayer Collection, Liverpool. Colchester and Liverpool Museums.

geometric patterns, and allows us to assign a relative, if not an absolute, date to the objects which bear it.

In the light of the evidence supplied by the Colchester grave, there can be little doubt that the style was evolved in or before the early part of the first century B.C., and good grounds seem to exist for believing that the latest specimens were made in the first half of the following century.[1] On that point some help is to be obtained from an examination of the material from the eastern counties.

Here at once we encounter the difficulty noted in the first chapter, namely, that there was no immigration on a large scale, corresponding to those of the west, or even apparently that of Yorkshire, unless it be up the Thames itself, until within a short time before the first landing of the Romans in 55 B.C.[2] Any settlement of that nature is to be connected with a group of Belgic people practising cremation, not, according to Bushe-Fox, the Belgae who later overran south and south-west Britain and were responsible for the consolidation, if not the foundation of Venta Belgarum and Calleva Atrebatum, but an earlier wave of that people, probably to be identified

---

[1] It cannot be too strongly stressed that the tendency, arising from over-reliance on associations like those of Birdlip and Nijmegen, to mark down the age of the generality of pieces engraved with flamboyant scrolled patterns against a basketry background is liable to breed an entire misconception of the development of Celtic design. In fact it implies an absolute negation of any orderly growth. The style occurs at Hunsbury and Bugthorpe in contexts and on forms that under no considerations whatever can be dated later than the first century B.C., and might even be earlier; subsequently it blossoms forth into its finest flowering, but by the beginning of the following century was already exhibiting signs of withering to its death. At the time of the deposition of the Nijmegen mirror, about A.D. 100, it may be said to have long been wiped off the map of Celtic ornament.

[2] J. P. Bushe-Fox, *Excavation of the Late-Celtic Urn-field at Swarling, Kent*, 30 ff.

with the British tribe of the Catuvellauni. To this
Belgic wave are assigned such cemeteries as Aylesford
and Swarling, Kent, and the whole class of cordoned,
pedestalled pottery which came from the Marne region
in Gaul. In this case we have at once direct evidence
of the origin of the new-comers, which, as noted above,
was rather lacking in the west, namely, objects which can
safely be dated to the first half of the first century B.C.,
exhibiting designs in which the palmette is still distinctly
visible.

Take, for example, the bronze-bound bucket from the
Aylesford grave published in 1899 by Sir Arthur Evans
(fig. 16).[1] There is nothing exactly comparable in British
work.[2] The Catherine-wheel motive and especially the
yin-yang scrolls are familiarly continental in their treatment; there is no embossed work of that character in
Britain. The same is even more true of the treatment of
the horses with their bifurcated, feathery tails, resembling
nothing so much as those of some Chinese goldfish. It
is not the horse of the British coins, but that of their
continental counterparts, and especially those of the
region from which the settlers came. The oenochoe and
patella from the same grave are certainly imports, so it
would hardly be surprising were the bucket to prove
equally of foreign fabric. The two first may be Italian,
as Sir Arthur Evans has said; but the bucket, if not
British, is undoubtedly Gallic work. But, import or no,
we still have the living remains of the palmette at hand
to serve as a model for future work; and thus it is that
in the eastern counties we meet with traces of its use at

[1] *Archaeologia*, lii. 360, fig. 11; *B.M. Guide* (*Iron Age*), 125, figs.
135–6.
[2] As his plate XIII serves to indicate.

a time when all remembrance of its meaning had entirely disappeared farther west. Good examples of this
are supplied by enamelled harness-mounts from Santon

FIG. 16. Bronze mounted bucket from Aylesford, Kent,
and details.

Downham[1] and Westhall, Suffolk.[2] From the former
site, one piece has the *yin-yang* double scroll carefully
reproduced in the enamel; on a second, the treatment
of the scrolls still retains some of the easy handling

[1] C. Fox, *Archaeology of the Cambridge Region*, cover.
[2] J. M. Kemble, *Horae Ferales*, pl. xx. 4.

found in its continental predecessors. Of the enamelled terrets from Westhall the largest has a poorly managed but unmistakable tendrilled scroll; the four smaller belonging to the same suite of harness are, however, much more jejune. They offer, in short, a good example of the rapid tendency to change, which, as we have seen, must have infected the western province. Here in the east we have the same process, and coming, as it does, nearer to historic times it allows its course to be traced with greater precision than in the other area.

But it suffered no better fate than in the west; and, if anything were needed to demonstrate how swiftly the remembrance of its meaning could be lost, it is here in the east, within a bare century, that the process can be clearly observed. Between Caesar's landing and the Claudian conquest the palmette and its scrolls as an intelligent interpretation of a classical loan had almost entirely disappeared, and Celtic art during that time received no fresh inspiration save that born of its own genius.

The course of its decadence can best be illustrated by various enamelled pieces of harness belonging to this period. A terret (pl. I. 3), formerly in the Fenton Collection and now in the Ashmolean Museum (probably from Suffolk), stands unquestionably at the top; the design is good and does not fall far short of the Westhall piece; after it must be placed those from Bapchild[1] and Richborough,[2] Kent, from Auchendolly,[3] Kirkcudbrightshire (undoubtedly manufactured in south-east Britain), and finally that from Runnymede,[4] Surrey. Among these

---

[1] *Proc. Soc. Ant.* xx. 57 and plate opp. [2] Unpublished.
[3] *Proc. Soc. Ant. Scot.* xx. 396, pl. VIII. 1.
[4] *Surrey Arch. Coll.* xxii. 198, pl. opp. p. 197, fig. III.

I. EARLY ENAMELS

1, 2, 4, 5, Polden Hill, Somerset ; 3, Suffolk ; 6, Westhall, Suffolk

Scale a little over one-half

last four it is difficult to decide to which, if any, should be accorded precedence in time. The Bapchild example is if anything the best conceived; between the other three there can be little choice. The same holds good of the three harness-mounts in the British Museum, two from Westhall (pl. 1. 6)[1] and one from London,[2] all of them with badly conceived and at the same time rather worrying patterns. This is in part due to the introduction of a secondary colour. It may be taken as a rule of pre-Roman enamel that the finest pieces that have come down to us are executed in a single colour, namely, red. The introduction of blue or yellow, at this stage always as spots, had a very detrimental effect upon the design. It is often said that one of the colours used was white; that is almost beyond question a mistake. I have carefully examined all the cases where white enamel is said to have been employed in pre-Roman times, and in every case the statement has proved to be wrong. Even the Westhall mount has been tested and found to fall into line; on it one spot which should, on the usual reckoning, be white actually has a large piece of blue visible in it, and experiment has shown that the 'white' is devitrified glass. This addition of spots of colour to contrast with the red is yet another sign of incipient decadence which comes out even more markedly in later enamel-work. It is, however, interesting to see how it began. The second colour does not appear in the eastern counties as enamel pure and simple, except on objects which also show signs of decadence in the ornamental design. In all the cases of blue employed as a secondary colour

[1] *Archaeologia*, xxxvi. 454, pl. xxxvii; J. M. Kemble, *Horae Ferales*, 195, pl. xix. 1.

[2] *Horae Ferales*, pl. xix. 2; also a fourth from Norton, Suffolk (ibid. pl. xix. 4), at Bury St. Edmunds.

on the group of horse-trappings examined above, the blue is not enamel like the red. The blue has been added in a curious manner, as illustrated by the Suffolk terret where in places it has broken out, thus allowing the bottom of the field which it was intended to fill to be examined. It seems that the whole of the design was filled in the first instance with material for red enamel, since it is easily distinguishable below the blue; and what is more surprising is that the blue is not enamel at all, but small pieces of blue glass, which appear to have been, as it were, cemented into position by the red enamel. At one point the red enamel can be seen to have oozed up between the blue glass and the bronze edge of the field. It is, in short, an experiment by a craftsman whose work was otherwise tolerably good.

In a boss from Hod Hill, Dorset,[1] now in the British Museum, the blue glass has been apparently set into the divisions it was intended to fill from the back, and subsequently secured in place by the red enamel which filled the remainder of the design. The edges of the divisions are slightly undercut, so that there was no danger of the filling falling out in front; but it would seem that the glass did not adhere to the metal in the same way as the red enamel, and therefore had to be backed by the more adhesive material.

The craft of enamelling as practised in Britain presents an interesting picture. As we have seen, it was extensively practised in the eastern counties in the century, or century and a half, before the Roman conquest. It had, however, been known in a simpler form for some time previously, but had then been employed principally in the form of

[1] The boss is illustrated in colour in Harmsworth's *Wonders of the Past*, 1216, fig. 6.

small studs, destined apparently, as on the Continent, to fill the place of the coral studs of an earlier age. Several cases of the use of coral are known in this country; for example, on fibulae from Arras, Yorkshire,[1] Harborough Cave, Derbyshire (fig. 17),[2] Newnham Croft,

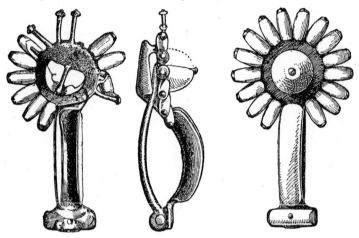

Fig. 17. Coral-mounted bronze fibula from Harborough Cave, Derbyshire.

Cambridge,[3] and Wood Eaton, Oxfordshire;[4] also on the wheel-shaped head of a swan-necked pin from Kilham, Yorkshire,[5] and apparently on another pin from the Thames, at Hammersmith;[6] and on a mount, whether part of harness or not it is difficult to decide, from Polden Hill, Somerset.[7] This last, as will appear shortly, must represent one of the latest occurrences of its use in Britain. But, as on the Continent, it was in time

[1] *Archaeologia*, lx. 267, fig. 13; 296, fig. 43; 298, fig. 46.
[2] *Proc. Soc. Ant.* xxii. 138, fig. 19.
[3] C. Fox, *Arch. Camb. Region*, pl. xviii. 2.
[4] *Oxfordshire Arch. Soc. Reports*, 1917, p. 93, fig. 3.
[5] *Archaeologia*, lx. 269, fig. 17.
[6] Ibid., lx. 270, fig. 18.   [7] Ibid. xiv, pl. xx. 2.

replaced by red enamel; the best instance of such sub-
stitution being the ornamental disk from Bugthorpe,
Yorkshire, with its ring of hemispherical bosses, secured
by pins riveted through their centres, clearly in imitation of the coral studs previously employed in a similar
manner.

Other methods of affixing enamel were also devised.
On the Battersea shield it is inset in cells formed of thin
strips of bronze arranged as a swastika within a circular
frame; on the Thames helmet the metal back of the
bosses is scored with cross-hatching to hold the enamel
in place. On certain small domed bosses—possibly
intended, like that accompanying the Thorpe sword[1]
(York Museum), to be affixed to the pommel of a sword—
it was secured, as can clearly be seen on a specimen from
Ixworth, Suffolk (Ashmolean Museum), by undercutting the edges of the open-work design of the bronze,
plugging the hollow interior with clay or other substance, and then filling the design from above with the
enamel. Here we are, however, reaching a comparatively
late period; the Thorpe sword belongs to the late
first century or the beginning of the second of our era,
while on the Ixworth boss the design is executed in a
manner reminiscent of the large fields in the ornamentation of the Old Warden mirror. A somewhat
earlier specimen of solid bronze from Beckley, Oxfordshire, decorated with four large spots, is also in the
Ashmolean Museum.

It has to be noted that all the early examples of the
use of enamel are on a small scale; not until shortly
before the Christian era is it used to decorate large

[1] *Archaeologia*, lx. 258, fig. 8; *Reliquary and Illustrated Archaeologist*,
xii. 269 and coloured plate opp. p. 217.

patterns in the champlevé technique, and that only in Britain. It would seem that the development of the craft along these lines must be set to the credit of the tribes who held south-east Britain from Kent to Suffolk in the period preceding the Roman conquest, and, if so, possibly to the Catuvellauni during their prime under their rulers from Tasciovanus to Cunobeline; the more so, as outside this region enamelling on so extensive a scale is hardly known. Indeed, there is only one instance of early pieces comparable in size and workmanship to the eastern productions, namely, those from a hoard found on Polden Hill, Somerset.

But, as the constituents of this hoard fully prove, the enamelling must have been executed by western craftsmen, who may admittedly have learnt the technique from farther east. The finest piece in the hoard (pl. 1. 4), possibly a harness-mount, is a masterpiece worthy to be set alongside the best of the engraved mirrors. It has the same flamboyant scrolls, drawn with the same sureness of hand to produce a design unrivalled by any of its eastern counterparts. More akin to these is another mount (pl. 1. 5); the form closely resembles that of some of the Suffolk specimens,[1] and like many of them its design shows a distinct decadence. The scroll-work is awkward and badly conceived, and the general effect is not improved by borders of little triangles. These, moreover, at once permit of its being regarded as a late piece; the same blend of scrolled patterns and triangles is used on the manifestly late mirror from Trelan Bahow, Cornwall (fig. 18), a further witness to the western

[1] The prototype of the form, however, belongs apparently to the western group: it is to be seen in comparatively diminutive examples (without enamel) at Hunsbury (T. J. George, *Hunsbury*, pl. 11, figs. 6 and 11).

fabrication of the Polden Hill enamels. Yet a third mount speaks in the same sense—an almost semicircular bronze plate with large curved notches in its straight edge and an openwork pattern below, and with large spots of enamel

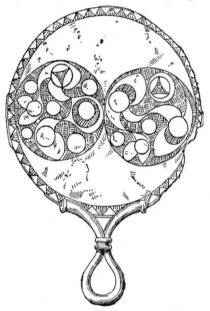

FIG. 18. Bronze engraved mirror from
Trelan Bahow, Cornwall.

surrounded by broad rings filled with transversely engraved lines, which, as shown above, are derived from the curved leaflets at the ends of earlier scrolls in this region.[1] This use of large spots of enamel takes us at once to the lipped terrets, of which the hoard contained no less than nineteen examples. Some of these are also decorated with spots, others with triangles, but the latter always with their sides adapted to the curve of the ring of the terret, never with perfectly straight sides

[1] *Archaeologia*, xiv, pl. XXII, fig. 3.

(pl. i. i). The enamelling was still subsidiary to the sense of line, not the inverse, as later becomes the case.

I propose to deal with these terrets more fully in another connexion; for the moment I may be allowed to anticipate that more detailed account so far as to state that these terrets with large lipped mouldings seem, as indicated by their distribution, to have been a conceit of western artificers. One with stiff, rather finicking little triangles was found at Alfriston, Sussex; otherwise, leaving on one side the Polden Hill hoard, we find ourselves in our search for terrets with similar mouldings, except for one rather late pair from Suffolk, once more following that age-long line of communication that runs from the Bristol Channel to Lincolnshire and Yorkshire. One from Leicester is identical with a Polden Hill variety; and out of four sets of harness from the hoard found at Stanwick, in the North Riding of Yorkshire, no less than three contain three to five terrets of the normal Polden Hill type, and one has in addition linchpins decorated with the same lipped mouldings; and on two of the sets practically every piece is similarly ornamented. Clearer evidence of some connexion—it may be purely cultural, it may have been political—between the two regions could hardly be demanded; and when we find in addition that a fragmentary bronze plate from Stanwick[1] has formed part of one identical with the segmental enamelled plate from Polden Hill, and even has an identically shaped opening, and the same disposition of the ornamentation, we need seek no further corroboration of close intercourse between them. After all, it has to be remembered that before the coming of the Romans the greater part of

[1] *Catalogue of Antiquities at Alnwick Castle*, 90, figs. 13 and 18.

southern England east of Devon was overrun by the second wave of Belgic invasion, and that some of its inhabitants may have fled northwards to escape the fate which it is thought befell such sites as Glastonbury at the hands of the new-comers.

Further evidence of the falling away which has been noted in certain of the enamels in the Polden Hill hoard is supplied by a series of objects which are held to have been the cheek-pieces of bridle-bits. On four, all of the same pattern, small triangles are combined with an amazon-shield motive,[1] such as frequently appears at this period, for example, on some of the eastern enamels, on an embossed bronze band in the Santon Downham hoard,[2] on the open-work mounts for a scabbard from Lambay Island, County Dublin,[3] and in combination with spots of enamel and lipped mouldings on the horn belonging to a crescentic type of terret from Weston-under-Penyard, Herefordshire,[4] the site of Ariconium under Roman rule (a complete terret of this form is among the objects in the Seven Sisters hoard; *infra*, p. 101). A fifth cheek-piece from Polden Hill is entirely decorated with triangles, recalling the Alfriston terret. All these last exhibit in one degree or another a tendency towards angularity in ornament, already foreshadowed by the curiously clumsy, hinged mount from Polden Hill,[5] one of the largest pieces of champlevé enamel that we possess from this period, though the enamel is now almost entirely wanting. The whole hoard, in short, provides an epitome of Celtic art in the

---

[1] *B.M. Guide* (*Iron Age*), 143, fig. 163.
[2] *Camb. Ant. Soc. Comm.*, xiii, pl. XVI. 1.
[3] *Proc. R. Irish Acad.* xxxviii, Sect. C, p. 243, pl. XXIV. 5.
[4] British Museum.
[5] *Archaeologia*, xiv. 92, pl. XXI, figs. 1–4.

west and its general trend in the last years of British freedom.

On a horn from Hod Hill, Dorset, similar to that from Weston-under-Penyard, the triangles have their sides curved in the same style as on the Polden Hill terrets.

The new impulse of which I have spoken above (p. 40) was in the nature of a discovery, of an invention. It is the outcome of the craftsman experimenting with his compasses in an endeavour to obtain novel effects and fresh combinations of curves. Something of the process can be observed in the series of bone trial-pieces found at Sliabh na Caillighe, Lough Crew, County Meath,[1] though there the artist did not quite reach the point attained by his fellow in Britain. That consisted in what may be termed breaking the back of the curve. Exactly the same phenomenon may be observed in Italy nearly a thousand years earlier. At some point the simple arched bow of the fibula ceased to give complete pleasure; the constant urge of novelty led to experiment, and as so often happens, when an attempt is made to get away from simplicity, it is apt to result in the bizarre. Here it was the fibula *a arco serpeggiante* (e.g. Montelius, *Civilisation Primitive en Italie*, I, serie A, 260), in which the middle of the bow was, as it were, crushed down, thus producing a bow with curves radiating from different centres and meeting each other at a sharp bend. In Britain there is some degree of spontaneity in its appearance; it emerges unconsciously out of the older system of pure fluent curves, for it is in the unintelligent products of the decadent period of the

---

[1] Eugene A. Cornwell, *Discovery of the Tomb of Ollamh Fodhla*, 52–6.

earlier geometrizing school that we can detect the steps by which, through a fresh grouping of the curves, the principle, once grasped, was brought into full activity, to become responsible for some of the boldest and most attractive decoration that Celtic art has ever produced.

And, as if it were a memory handed down through the ages, the Celts in Britain launched forth on exactly the same experiment on their own fibulae with an exactly similar result. Dr. Cyril Fox has illustrated most of the known examples,[1] though he omits one of the most interesting, a second specimen from Arras, figured by Greenwell,[2] and shows how it started from a fibula of la Tène I form with a heavy knob on the foot and an ingenious tubular hinge. In other fibulae with the same type of hinge the back of the bow has been broken down, producing what Sir Arthur Evans has named the involuted type. Their diffusion from Wiltshire and Oxfordshire (fig. 19) to Yorkshire once more, as Dr. Fox points out, furnishes a series of milestones along the same route as before, and in the same direction from south-west to north-east. Which particular school in Britain saw the first application of the principle it would be difficult to say. Quite possibly it falls to the credit of the western school, both by reason of the distribution of the fibulae so treated and also because the earlier examples of its use all seem to emanate from that area; not until it reaches a more advanced stage does it make its appearance farther east. But, so far as I am able to discover, the western school does not appear to have adapted the same principle to decoration on a flat surface;

[1] *Arch. Cambrensis*, 1927, pp. 93 and 95.
[2] *Archaeologia*, lx. 267, fig. 13.

that is to say, with them it is an architectonic device, not a subtle transformation of linear design.

In dealing with the mirrors I have endeavoured to explain the considerations which should govern their

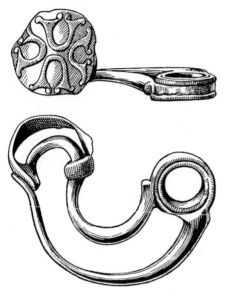

FIG. 19. Bronze fibula from Beckley, Oxon.

chronological classification, partly based upon the form of the handle and partly on the deterioration and changes in the decoration. Examples like those from Old Warden and that in the Disney Collection in the British Museum[1] may, from the latter aspect, almost be ranked as complete failures; but that from Billericay and the Mayer (R. Thames?) specimen stand on another footing (fig. 15). The latter, as already indicated, by reason of the disposition of the ornament in circles, has to be placed

[1] Ibid. lxi, 339, fig. 7. The Gibbs collection specimen, probably from Kent (ibid. 340, fig. 8), shows a more balanced treatment, but with the broken-backed curve in full use.

late; and the former is only redeemed by the tripartite balance of its clumsy design. Now on both these mirrors the broken-backed treatment of curves can be clearly detected, though still employed in a somewhat halting manner that suggests an experimental stage.

By contrast, on an enamelled harness-mount from Canterbury it has been adapted to the object with extraordinary success. This mount, now in the British Museum, is here figured fully restored (pl. II. 3). In its present state it is but a sad wreck of its original glory, but fortunately the whole composition of the design can still be clearly distinguished, and, as the restoration shows, it can claim—even if somewhat bizarre, yet in the breadth of its conception and the boldness of its execution in large contrasted masses of colour, free from the finicking tiresomeness of the spotted examples—to be one of the most striking and splendid specimens of enamelling produced during this early Celtic epoch in Britain.

Here and there we meet with the same treatment applied to bands of thin bronze embossed with cleverly designed and carefully executed scroll-work. Notable examples are those from Rodborough Common, near Stroud, Gloucestershire,[1] and a closely analogous example from Stanfordbury, Bedfordshire,[2] and lastly, associated with amazon-shield motives, on a band from the Santon Downham hoard[3] which contained the enamelled plates already described. This hoard, like the contents of the vault at Stanfordbury, included several objects of Roman, or Roman provincial, origin, all of types that can be dated to a period before the

---

[1] *B.M. Guide (Iron Age)*, 146, fig. 169.
[2] C. Fox, *Arch. Camb. Region*, pl. XVIII. 4.
[3] *Cambs. Ant. Soc. Proc. and Comm.* xiii. 153, pl. XVI. 1.

Roman conquest, even if also known from finds of a later date. It may be doubted whether any of the richly furnished tombs, like those at Welwyn or Stanfordbury, are later than the conquest; they would seem rather to represent the wealth of imports that was reaching Britain in the hey-day of Celtic prosperity. Though the date of deposition of the Santon Downham hoard might be subsequent to the conquest and possibly a result of it, its contents are too similar to those from Welwyn and Stanfordbury to be separated from them in time.

But even though these first attempts are in time not far removed from that of the Claudian invasion, they have little or no future in southern England. It is on the fringe of the first stages of the Roman conquest that we have to look for its further development, and it is greatly to be deplored that the British were not spared from invasion long enough to enable them to realize it to the full. As it is, we cannot be too grateful that we have left to us a few examples of that development, sufficient, alas! to indicate how much we must have lost.

The outstanding witnesses to its beauty are the Trawsfynydd tankard (fig. 20 a)[1] and the torc from Lochar Moss.[2] The former, now in Liverpool Museum, has in its handle one of the most beautiful things in Celtic art; simplicity, elegance, and balance, all combine to render it wholly satisfying. Romilly Allen has likened it to a piece of Gothic tracery and has even said, 'It may be looked upon as a blasphemous anticipation of Christian art by the pagan Celt'. This is a little hard on the pagan Celt. For to him is due all the credit for having by his own genius created such beauty. I doubt whether in

[1] R. E. M. Wheeler, *Prehistoric and Roman Wales*, 210, fig. 85.
[2] *B.M. Guide (Iron Age)*, 158, fig. 188.

the whole of Gothic art the exquisite treatment of the mouldings has ever been surpassed.

The handle shows a detail which comes much into evidence on the pieces of this school, namely, the hemispherical boss in the centre of the roundels. It recurs continually, so much so that we can almost speak of a period of 'boss' decoration. Possibly it is the outcome of the introduction of spots into the enamels of the eastern counties, for example, on the Bapchild terret, but it has to be remembered that in enamels of the western school the spot is a commonplace of ornament. It is not, however, until we reach the period of the broken-backed curve that it is used to the best advantage, and then perhaps chiefly because we find it in the moulded form where the glint of the metal enhances its effectiveness.

On the analogy of the roundels on the Trawsfynydd tankard we can place here a group of open-work roundels with a shank at the back, mostly decorated with a triskele design; such are known from Berkshire (British Museum) (fig. 21 c) and Seamill, Ayrshire (National Museum of Scottish Antiquities, Edinburgh),[1] and in a repoussé variant from Kingsholm, Gloucestershire (Ashmolean Museum),[2] all with a central boss. The same boss is used effectively on the repoussé bronze bands from Rodborough Common, near Stroud, Gloucestershire, and in quite another manner and somewhat later on the scabbards from Cotterdale, Yorkshire,[3] and from Mortonhall, Pentland, near Edinburgh (fig. 32 a),[4] two of those

[1] Archaeological and Historical Collections of Ayr and Wigton, iii. 63, fig. 3.
[2] James Douglas, Nenia Britannica, 134, pl. XXVII. 1. A variant form of smaller size (fig. 21 b) comes from Brighthampton or Stanlake (British Museum). [3] B.M. Guide (Iron Age), pl. IX. 9.
[4] Cat. Nat. Mus. Scottish Ant., 1892, FA. 35.

Fig. 20. (a) Detail of bronze tankard-handle from Trawsfynydd, Merioneth (c. ⅔). Liverpool Museum. (b) Enamelled bronze mount from Chepstow, Monmouthshire (p. 98) (c. ¾). Private. (c) Gilt bronze fibula from Aesica, Northumberland (p. 109) (c. ¾). Newcastle Museum.

scabbards with bifurcated chapes and the strap-band placed at the middle of the scabbard, which with those from Stanwick[1] and Flasby,[2] Yorkshire, Sadberge,

FIG. 21. Examples of incipient 'boss' style. (*a*) Wood Eaton, Oxon; (*b*) Stanlake, Oxon; (*c*) Berkshire.

Durham,[3] and Worton, Lancashire,[4] are of the type assigned by Déchelette to his la Tène IV. They may all be dated to about A.D. 50.

Among other interesting products of this style is the

[1] *Catalogue of Antiquities at Alnwick Castle*, 88 and 90, figs. 6–7; J. M. Kemble, *Horae Ferales*, 193, pl. XVIII. 2.

[2] *Proc. Arch. Inst.* (York, 1846), 11, pl. V, 1.

[3] *Proc. Soc. Ant.* xvi. 4–6 and fig.

[4] *Horae Ferales*, 192, pl. XVIII. 1; *B.M. Guide (Iron Age)*, 108, fig. 117.

half of a torc from Llandyssul, Cardiganshire,[1] now in
Bristol Museum. Here the curves run with greater
freedom, and the break seems to be masked by the leaf-
like motive enclosing a large boss, the same idea, here
treated in relief, that we find on the mirrors and the
Canterbury enamelled mount. On an openwork
disk, moulded in front and flat behind (its use and
its provenance are unknown; it has been long in the
Ashmolean), composed of an outer ring filled with a
triskele design, the curves are stiffer and the large inter-
spaces are of a form that one also meets with on the
mirrors and the enamelled mount; it has also the leaves
with a large boss within them, but here the bosses have
been made of some extraneous substance, perhaps coral,
as apparently is the case on the Polden Hill mount.[2]
Alternatives are possible; enamel as on the Bugthorpe
boss,[3] amber or glass as on the Datchet fibula,[4] or even
stone like the sections of encrinite-stems on a mount
from Northamptonshire[5] or the piece of breccia (?) on
one of the Arras armlets.[6] Reference to the Polden Hill
hoard gives us at once the position of the rectangular
plate from Moel Hiraddug, Flintshire,[7] with its interesting flamboyant scrolls (fig. 22), analogous to those on
the fine Polden Hill enamel and the Birdlip and
Desborough mirrors, interesting because they have
reached the point at which the principle of the break is
just about to come to a head. The Hiraddug plate also

[1] R. E. M. Wheeler, *Prehistoric and Roman Wales*, 211, fig. 86.
[2] *Archaeologia*, xiv, 92, pl. xx. 2.
[3] *B.M. Guide (Iron Age)*, 114, 125.
[4] *Proc. Soc. Ant.* xv. 191 and coloured plate.
[5] Ibid. xvii. 166.
[6] *Archaeologia*, lx. 299; York Museum, W. 43.
[7] *Arch. Cambr.* 1928, p. 283, fig. 16.

FIG. 22. Embossed bronze plate from Moel Hiraddug, Flintshire (c $\frac{2}{3}$).
Welshpool Museum.

possesses a feature which first comes into common use at this period—though foreshadowed on the Birdlip mirror—that is, in the relief given to the monotony of a uniform border-moulding by enlarging it trumpet-wise from two directions to a transverse ridge, here repeated thrice round the circumference of the circle to match the threefold disposition of the central design.[1]

Another group of antiquities falling into the same general period and style are those curious spoon-like objects, which are known by no less than two pairs (Weston, near Bath,[2] and Crosby Ravensworth, West-morland[3]) and two single specimens (London[4] and the Thames[5]) from England, a pair from Scotland (Burn-mouth, Berwickshire),[6] and two from Wales (Castell Nadolig, Penbryn, Cardiganshire,[7] and Llanfair, Den-bighshire[8]); lastly, two pairs and a single example from unrecorded sites in Ireland.[9] Their general date is provided by the presence of the hatched terminal curl of a scroll on one of the Burnmouth spoons, like those noted above (p. 30) on the mirrors and on a mount from Polden Hill (p. 46). On the back of the handles of one from Weston, amid delicate scroll-work, the broken-backed curve is plainly visible (fig. 23 *a*), and again in a

---

[1] I cannot possibly assent to the opinion expressed by Mr. Hawkes (T. D. Kendrick and C. F. C. Hawkes, *Archaeology in Great Britain*, 1914–31, p. 186) that this plate dates from the second century B.C. It can hardly be earlier than the close of the first century B.C.

[2] *Arch. Journ.* xxvi. 61, fig. 8.

[3] *B.M. Guide (Iron Age)*, 148, fig. 174.

[4] *Arch. Journ.* xxvi. 55, fig. 2.

[5] Ibid. 54, fig. 1.

[6] *Archaeologia*, lxxvii. 106, fig. 11.

[7] *Arch. Journ.* xxvi. 58, figs. 5–6; R. E. M. Wheeler, op. cit., fig. 88.

[8] Ibid. 56, figs. 3–4.

[9] Ibid. 64–7, figs. 11–15.

weak form on those from Crosby Ravensworth. On others, as those from the Thames and Penbryn, the

a

b

Fig. 23. Details of ornament on (*a*) bronze spoons from Weston, Somerset; (*b*) bronze axle-cap from R. Thames, Brentford.

bossed decoration comes to the fore. The Weston pair shows how the Celt at times allowed full play to his fancy; the designs on the two spoons are not identical. In character they recall those on a bronze axle from the Thames in the Layton Collection in Brentford Public Library (fig.

a

b   *c*

FIG. 24. (*a*) Embossed bronze plaque from Lambay Island,
Co. Dublin, Ireland ($\frac{4}{7}$). National Museum of Ireland. (*b*) Restoration of design on plaque. (*c*) Rock-carving at Ilkley, Yorkshire.

23 *b*),[1] though here the regularity of the design and the clear traces of the palmette may argue for an earlier date.

We see the process of the broken scroll just beginning on the Wraxall torc;[2] it can be observed on what for convenience I may call the south-west quadrant of its circle; and if, as appears probable, the holes in this torc were originally filled with enamel, we have at once the origin of certain bosses in the bronze itself which characterize the more advanced products of the broken-backed curve. A poorer effort along similar lines, in my opinion certainly earlier than the association with a Samian bowl might suggest, is the torc from the Isle of Portland, Dorset; here, apparently, enamel was not used and the holes were left empty.[3]

The broken-backed curve or scroll occurs again on the embossed disk found on Lambay Island, off the coast of County Dublin (fig. 24 *a–b*).[4] The design is simple enough, being composed of a triquetral motive, carried out in narrow embossed lines, in a manner somewhat reminiscent of those on the Llandyssul torc; at the centre is riveted an embossed rosette, and the tip of each arm is prolonged in a rather aimless scroll terminating in a roundel with two spots. It is of importance since it was found in association with fibulae, two of them of the Roman provincial thistle-type,[5] a form in vogue from

---

[1] *Archaeologia*, lix. 22, fig. 22.   [2] Ibid. liv. 495, pl. XLVIII.

[3] *B.M. Guide (Iron Age)*, 151, fig. 176. Confirmation of the date of these torcs is furnished by an imperfect specimen, found in or near Dorchester (Dorchester Museum), engraved with flamboyant patterns in the style of the Polden Hill mount (pl. I. 2).

[4] *Proc. R. Irish Acad.* xxxviii, Sect. C, p. 243, pl. XXIV. I.

[5] T. D. Kendrick and C. F. C. Hawkes, op. cit. 203. On comparison with the Lambay Island disk the svastika-like rock-carving at Ilkley, W. Riding, Yorkshire (fig. 24 *c*), with its aimless scroll springing from the end of one of the arms falls chronologically at once into its place. (J. R. Allen, *Celtic Art*, 58; F. & H. Elgee, *Yorkshire*, 112, pl. III).

c. A.D. 25 to 50, and another of British first-century form, thus suggesting a date for their deposition about, or possibly rather later than, the middle of the century. This accords with the usual dating adopted for torcs strung with moulded bronze beads, such as also accompanied this find. Others of the same class are known

FIG. 25. Embossed plate on bronze mirror from
Balmaclellan, Dumfriesshire.

from Embsay, Yorkshire,[1] Lamberton Moor, Berwickshire[2]—the latter in an association which would place it in the early part of the second century, though it need not itself be so late—and finally the beautiful torc from Lochar Moss, Dumfriesshire.[3] On this torc the broken-backed curve, again in combination with spots or bosses, is carried a stage farther than on its Llandyssul fellow, inasmuch as, in addition to the break at each boss, the scrolls are also broken in the interval between them. As a running design, it makes up in cleverness for what it lacks in grace; but there is present that touch of the bizarre to which Celtic design at all periods seems to have been somewhat prone.

[1] *Archaeologia*, xxxi. 517, pl. XXIII.
[2] *Proc. Soc. Ant. Scot.* xxxix. 367, fig. 1.
[3] *Archaeologia*, xxxiv. 83, pl. XI; *B.M. Guide (Iron Age)*, 157, fig. 188.

Lastly, in the north the broken-backed scroll in a simpler form is used to decorate the mirror found at Balmaclellan, Dumfriesshire (fig. 25).[1] This mirror is probably the latest of its class, though associated, as noted above, with basketry engraving of a somewhat earlier style. Doubtless many products of southern schools found their way northwards into the safe retreat of Galloway, in whose fastnesses the Celts took refuge, much as did the Covenanters of a later age. The Auchendolly enamelled terret and the enamelled cheek-piece found at Easter Wooden Farm, Eckford, Roxburghshire,[2] followed the same road.

We have now to retrace our steps for a moment to the earlier part of the first century of our era before passing on to the story of Celtic ornament in Roman times. On some of the mirrors, especially the later examples, we encounter, in addition to the single detached ring referred to on more than one occasion above, another unconnected motive, also circular and similarly shaded, but with a pair of plain roundels side by side within it. It is well seen on the Billericay mirror and on the spear from the Thames[3] accompanied by basketry shading. This motive was developed and employed in a variety of ways on late pre-Roman work. It occurs, for instance, on a bracelet from one of the group of graves on Stamford Hill, Plymouth,[4] on which the 'eyed' roundels are linked together by scrolls. It can be faintly detected on a fragment of thin repoussé bronze from Ham Hill, Somerset, in the Walter Collection in Taunton Museum,[5]

[1] J. Anderson, *Scotland in Pagan Times* (*Iron Age*), 127, fig. 104.
[2] *Proc. Soc. Ant. Scot.* lxvi. 365, fig. 49.
[3] *Man*, 1931, 182.
[4] *Archaeologia*, xl. 502, pl. xxxi. 2.
[5] *V. C. H. Somerset*, i. 296, fig. 63, 4.

and very clearly on the torc from Trenoweth, Cornwall,[1] in which case the holes have been filled with coloured glass. On this torc the motive is combined with a border of triangles after the manner of the mirror from Trelan Bahow in the same county.[2] The same motive is employed to decorate the terminal disk on the foot of a broken-backed fibula from Wood Eaton, Oxfordshire.

To sum up, Celtic art at this period contained within it all the seeds of a rapid and complete decay; it was breaking up on the rocks of petty details. In the broken-backed curve it was in danger of losing all its former command over the purity of curving line, though retaining some elements of a possible future. Of the other two the 'eyed' disk appeared for a short while longer, but the fashion of triangles, the return to primitive ornament, was destined to exercise its influence particularly in southern Britain for many years to come. Only in the north did Celtic art henceforward show any signs of real life; and it is there that we shall eventually have to follow the course of its struggle for existence.

[1] *Archaeologia*, xvi. 137, pl. x. A fragment of a torc similarly ornamented is among the finds from Greenhill, at Weymouth, Dorset (British Museum), also with glass fillings.

[2] *Oxfordshire Arch. Soc. Reports*, 1917, p. 94, pl. 1 *f*.

III

EARLY BRITISH NUMISMATIC ART

NUMISMATIC art is one of the later ventures of the British craftsman. It is difficult to say exactly at what period the first coins were struck in this country. Many of those found on British soil and assigned in the past to British mints have now been relegated to a foreign source. Such are those illustrated by Sir John Evans in plate A of his uninscribed series, now recognized as emanating from the Bellovaci of Normandy; and, more important still, his plate B, nos. 1–6, have now to be dropped from the tale of purely British coins, since they belong of right to the tribes of north-eastern Gaul, such as the Atrebates, Morini, and the like.[1] There are others besides; certain of the small coins of the class illustrated in Evans's plate E, nos. 9–11, also belong to Gaulish mints. In the very nature of things it could hardly be otherwise. In the close contact established between Gaul and Britain during the period of almost continuous migration, Gaulish coins would be bound to find their way to this country by way of commerce or by actual transference by the immigrants themselves. It could hardly be expected that every coin found in Britain was actually minted there. As is now known, this was certainly not so, though it might be hazardous to assert in the face of the migrations themselves that the same types were not actually struck on both sides of the Channel.

The great hoard of gold coins found in Whaddon Chase, Buckinghamshire, in 1849, comprised numerous examples (judging from the known specimens, for the

[1] *Rev. Num. Belge*, 1864, pp. 1 ff.

hoard was dispersed into many hands after its discovery), indeed almost a preponderance of types, which, as noted above, are those assigned to the Atrebates or Morini. But, when it is remembered that the tribe, to whom is to be attributed the founding of the Catuvellaunian hegemony based in the first place on Verulamium and later under Cunobeline on Camulodunum, is now regarded as an initial wave of Belgic or closely kindred people, associated in archaeology with cordoned pottery and cremation-burial, it is not unlikely that continental types were struck here.

The particular series of coins, however, which it would seem should be associated with the transplantation of this new culture into Britain are actually those usually assigned to the Bellovaci. It is recognized that the new phase makes its appearance about the beginning of the first century B.C., and it is to the same period that these Gaulish coins are attributed by French numismatists. They can hardly be later, for the series that succeeds them in Britain before the Roman conquest is too large to allow it and the Bellovaci coins found in Britain to be crowded into a shorter period. That they stand at the head of the coins found in this country is shown by their closer proximity to the original Philippic stater than any other British coin types.

It is possible to argue that they are all importations by way of commerce; but with such constant immigration in progress, as was the case in the centuries before Christ, it is just as likely that they were brought into the country by invaders, if not actually minted here after Gaulish models for use after their arrival. In either case the important point is their distribution, which closely coincides with that of the cordoned pottery and cremation, that is to say, on the coasts of Kent, Essex, and southern Suffolk, and the south bank of the Thames together with some extension into Middlesex and Hertfordshire. Outside these a few strays come from the Sussex coast; otherwise only in the far west from Karn Bré, Cornwall, clearly in connexion with the tin trade. Their weight is much higher than that of any other coins in Britain, whether imported or not, and from the subsequent history of British coinage in the districts where they occur it becomes evident that they were not current for very long. Their treatment of the imitation of the Philippic stater is of a specialized character which finds no echo in any of the later issues. These, as will be seen, are for the most part based on a continental type different alike in treatment of the design and in weight.

If it is legitimate to draw any conclusions of an historical nature from this change, it must mean that a first immigration of tribes from the Seine region was followed by others, more powerful, occupying more easterly districts. It may be that the tribes issuing coins of the Bellovaci type were originally themselves situated farther east and that they were displaced by the gradual spread westwards of others more preponderantly Belgic, though culturally closely akin to those whom they had displaced. In that case the cultural differences between them would be of a somewhat shadowy kind, and would render it difficult to draw any marked distinction between them, at least during the period of the earlier issues of coins in eastern Britain.

The statement of Messrs. Hawkes and Dunning in 'The Belgae of Gaul and Britain'[1] that, while 'pedestal

---

[1] *Archaeological Journal*, lxxxvii. 232.

urns of the Marne type are plentiful in the country of the Caleti and Veliocasses, . . . nothing of the sort is attributable to the Bellovaci', is not of great significance, since it is not proven that the territory of the Bellovaci of Caesar's day is identical with that of the period to which the coins belong. The gradual movement westwards of Belgic tribes had been in progress for a long time previously. The coins are found in the districts inhabited by the Bellovaci of the *Commentaries*, but that does not necessarily mean that they were actually minted by that tribe. They might equally well belong to others like the Caleti and Veliocasses, who had themselves in turn displaced tribes by whom the coins generally attributed to them had been struck. In short, the conditions of Caesar's day are not a criterion by which one is entitled to judge those of fifty years previously.

The important point in any case is that the whole of the earliest British coinage starts from types which were struck by tribes inhabiting the regions comprised within the territories of Caesar's Belgae, whether they were in the first instance coined by Belgae or not. Of these coins the earliest typologically are the Bellovaci types, as is shown by the obverses, where the locks of hair on the Apollo-head are indicated by tasselled curves, such as persist on varieties found at points farther inland in Britain than any reached by the majority of the Bellovaci types, down to a time when all resemblance to a human head is passing out of existence.

The Bellovaci coins seem, then, to be the first actually current in Britain; but it is such types as are included in the Whaddon Chase hoard that represent the marked change in style to which I have just alluded. If the Bellovaci coins are to be equated with the initiation of the culture of the cordoned pottery and the rite of cremation, and are held to be imported continental issues, then we must agree with Mr. Bushe-Fox's contention[1] that not only were no coins struck in Britain before 100 B.C., but in all probability for several decades after.

Such a series as the Whaddon Chase hoard offers a convenient starting-point for a consideration of the Briton as a numismatic artist. The general type is still the well-known one of the stater of Philip of Macedon, by this time reduced to a mere travesty, particularly on the obverse: the face of Apollo so mangled and distorted that little remains except an exaggerated band representing the laurel-wreath, flanked by a jumble of tasselled hooks, remains of the locks of hair, or by crescentic figures, outlines of the prominent portions in the moulding of the cheek, mouth, and chin. The reverse had suffered but little better; the biga reduced to a single horse, and a single wheel, roundel, or rosette replacing the chariot, while the victory had lost all meaning in a medley of strokes and dashes, merely serving as 'fill-ups' in the field.

With such models before them, it would be strange indeed if early British numismatic history should not be proved to have been one of absolute failure, but that is not the case. From the outset it is remarkable how, within the limitations which, save in a few rare instances, seem to have hedged round numismatic art for long periods at a time, the British quickly struck out into new paths, none, it is true, of great daring or merit, nor in any degree comparable with those attained in other

[1] J. P. Bushe-Fox, *Excavations of the Late-Celtic Urn-field at Swarling*, 36.

artistic fields, but nevertheless illustrative of the same independence of artistic spirit.

The first coinage, in short, belongs to the period immediately preceding, if not contemporary with, the advance of Rome into Gaul and the severance of the Celts from all new artistic impulses save those derived from their future masters. The Celts in Britain, in particular, were thrown back on their own resources of invention; they had to make the best of the little material they possessed, and it is thus that the British coinage presents certain features that, as it were, stamp it with the hall-marks of its artists' efforts to fashion something new from an intractable and unpromising material.

Associated with the continental types in the Whaddon Chase hoard was one other at least that has an undoubted claim to be regarded as purely British. It has a perfectly plain obverse, and in this respect resembles the whole group of coins attributed to the Morini by Hermand in 1864,[1] but on the reverse is a quite spirited representation of the horse. It is not, as on other coins of the hoard, depicted with a rat-like tail, or even devoid of such and merely provided with a rabbit-like scut set high on the animal's rump (e.g. coins of the Morini), fashioned from one of the meaningless 'fill-ups' floating in thin air above the horse's back on the continental types. Of this, the coin from Elham, Kent (formerly in Sir John Evans's collection and assigned by him to his type pl. B. 8), is an especially good example. Its exergual ornament of a bar surmounting a row of torc-like semicircles, each enclosing a dot and arranged alternately up and down, in itself the forerunner of a continuous zigzag band with dots in each angle,

[1] *Rev. Num. Belge*, 1864, pl. XII.

occurs in the same combination on coins of the Morini.

The British version of the horse has a noble triple tail, a type which recurs on a long series of British coins, and marks it as peculiarly British. It is true that it does occur on coins speculatively attributed to the Remi, but that seems to be the only continental appearance of this peculiarity. The distribution of the British coins bearing this horse is, moreover, such as to admit of little doubt that it was a production of the western group, but, as will be seen later, under influences from the eastern group. Naturally it is impossible to date the uninscribed series with any certainty, but the combination of types in the Whaddon Chase hoard does afford presumptive evidence that for the most part they precede any of the inscribed series. Nevertheless, not by much. The earliest of the inscribed coins, those of Commius (Evans, pl. I. 10)—a ruler whom we know to have been contemporary with Caesar's invasion—of his son Tincommius, and Tasciovanus, son of Cassivellaunus, the presumed founder of the Catuvellaunian house in Britain, differ in their reverses so little from the uninscribed examples that it may fairly be assumed that the latter, as found at Whaddon Chase, were struck for Tasciovanus himself, if not for his father. The latter is the more probable, since the series of coins bearing Tasciovanus's name, or plausibly connected with Verulamium, his capital, is large and varied enough as it is to cover the period of thirty-five years between 40 and 5 B.C. assigned to his reign, without adding many others to the list;[1] and more so, since he had the example of the

---

[1] There are a few which have better claims to be assigned to this ruler.

somewhat earlier Commius for the addition of an inscription on what at any rate must be the first of a long series that bears his name.

The triple-tailed horse recurs on coins of Boduoc, belonging to an area roughly coinciding with Oxfordshire, north Berkshire, and Gloucestershire, on those of the Catti and others bearing the names COMVX, EISV, or VOCORIO-AD from still farther west, and also on coins bearing the name ANTED (Antedrigus). For this reason alone, apart from their distribution, it is impossible to assent to Sir John's identification of this Antedrigus with the ruler whose name appears on some of the coins of the Iceni. The latter in any case are totally different in character; and even the explanation of his expulsion from East Anglia and establishment in the west is particularly unsatisfying, for, as I hope to show later, the Icenian types, among which those of Antedrigus from East Anglia are to be counted, must be considerably later in date, and, if they had to be associated with the western chieftain at all, would tell a story of movement by him in exactly the reverse direction to that which Sir John Evans has pictured. An additional fact to be taken into consideration is the appearance of the name ANTED also on smaller coins of a peculiar type shared alike by COMVX, EISV, and VOCORIO-AD, all unquestionably rulers of western origin, and all issuing coins of the larger module, in the same style as the larger ANTED coins from the same area.

One of the most striking features of the British gold coinage is its conservatism. With the exception of some five examples, mostly of small module, and also forming part of the inscribed series, throughout its history the gold coinage remains faithful to the prototype of the

Philippic stater.[1] On all, the horse still serves as
the reverse type. No vital change is made. At times
the animal is sadly disjointed, almost to the point of
becoming unrecognizable, but the remnants are nevertheless the horse, accompanied by the usual 'fill-ups', dis-
integrated remains of the chariot, the victory, and other
details. Here the process of copying from already debased originals allowed no scope for intelligent appreciation or inspiration to flights of creative fancy. By
the time the need of something better was felt, the
Briton had access to the issues of Roman mints, and
adopted new models, producing some amazingly spirited
efforts. The horseman of Tasciovanus, brandishing his
carnyx in place of a lance, and other equally satisfying
pieces come immediately to mind.

But the story of the obverse stands on another plane.
Coins exist with obverses plain except for a sunk panel
stamped with a legend, BODVOC, TINC, or the like;
though even these, as coins of Tasciovanus (e.g. Evans,
pl. VIII. 6–7) suggest, may be merely copies of the label
adopted for some of his later issues. Leaving these aside,
a coin of Verica with a branch between the letters of the
legend is, strictly speaking, the sole gold coin on which
an adventitious device is introduced. The origin of
this motive is not without interest. It would seem to
have been inspired by coins of Augustus struck in Gaul,
17–15 B.C., on which are two olive-branches flanking
the legend.[2] No other coin of the period seems to compare so closely.

For the rest, difficult though it may seem to believe,

---

[1] I exclude a group of doubtful pieces, such as pl. E. 6–12, of types
struck on both sides of the Channel.

[2] H. A. Grueber, *Roman Republican Coins*, ii. 423–4, pl. CVI, 16.

the obverses one and all belong to a continuous series, illustrating the evolution of the design the meaning of which, by the time it reached these shores, was in process of being rapidly forgotten. Coins with still intelligible heads were passing from the Continent to Britain by way of commerce; but on the models from which the preponderance of British coins took their being, namely, those of the Atrebates and Morini in north-eastern Gaul, the head had already reached so advanced a stage of unintelligent copying as to deprive it of even the little chance retained by the horse on the reverse, of its nature being still comprehended once it had left its original home.

Thus it comes about that the obverse type shows greater variety, and at the same time illustrates once more how the Celt in Britain proceeded to devise something fresh. But there is still the trait of conservatism, suggesting that the gold coinage was almost regarded as sacrosanct, and that any wide deviation from the prototype was a thing to be seriously avoided. All that the moneyers could do was to make some attempt to reduce the design to a more orderly condition. But since their improved designs were almost invariably engraved on a die larger than the flan to which it was applied, it seldom happens that their improvements meet with great success. The accompanying diagram will serve to indicate the lines along which the changes proceeded (fig. 26).

The uppermost coin is beyond question an importation from Gaul, a gold stater of 90 grains, actually a low weight for the type which can attain to as much as 94 to 96 grains. Here the features of the face have become sadly blurred, but the indication of the nose and mouth

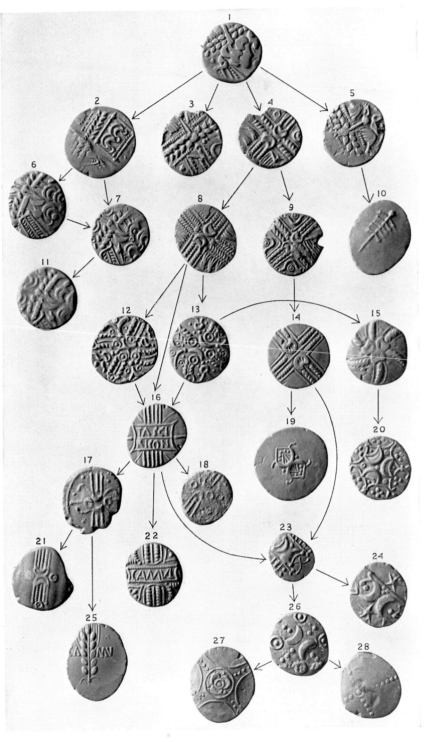

FIG. 26. Evolution of design on British gold coins.
British Museum.

KEY TO PLATE 26

					Grains.
1.	B 7	Uninscribed	Kent	AV	90
2.	C 6	,,	(?)	AV	c. 90
3.	C 7	,,	Whaddon Chase	AV	c. 90
4.	C 9	,,	,, ,,	AV	87
5.	C 5	,,	,, ,,	AV	90
6.	B 9	,, (triple tail)	,, ,,	AV	90
7.	⌈D 5 or ⌊I 10	Commius ,, ,,	(?)	AV	83
8.	D 7	Uninscribed	Surrey	AV	83
9.	XIII 13	MOD	Lincolnshire	AV	..
10.	I 7	⌈Antedrigus, Comux ⟨Catti, &c. ⌊(triple tail)	W. England	AV	69–83
11.	I 12	Tincommius	..	AV	83½
12.	V 9	Tasciovanus	..	AV	c. 83
13.	V 10	,,	..	AV	85
14.	XIV 9	Addedomaros	..	AV	85
15.	XIV 5	,,	..	AV	84¼
16.	VIII 7	Tasciovanus (TASCIO- RIGON)	..	AV	c. 83
17.	XXI 2	,,	(VER)	AE	..
18.	VIII 5	,,	,, ..	AE	..
19.	XVI 1	Addedomaros	..	AV	84–6
20.	XVIII 2	Antedrigus (eastern)	..	AV	79¼
21.	IV 9	Dubnovellaunus	..	AV	81–6
22.	IX 1	Cunobelinus (CAMV)	..	AV	c. 83–5
23.	XV 3	Antedrigus & Iceni	..	AR	..
24.	XIV 10	Iceni	..	AV	82
25.	IX 6	Cunobelinus (CAMV)	..	AV	83¼
26.	XIV 11	Iceni	..	AV	83½
27.	XXIII 3	,,	..	AV	83½
28.	XXIII 6	,,	..	AV	86

is still recognizable. The second row consists of coins from the Whaddon Chase hoard itself, or of types found in that hoard. In all, the face has disappeared; the curious left-hand piece has a feature which occurs in somewhat different guise on Gaulish coins and has won for them the name of *monnaies à l'epsilon*,[1] obviously due to the merger of the two front crescentic locks of hair with the points representing the forehead, nose, and chin respectively. But clearly the head is here in process of passing into a purely cruciform arrangement, the constituent elements of which are the laurel-wreath balanced by the hair on the one side and by survivals from the details of the face on the other. In no. 4 the cruciform character has advanced a further step. It is to be noted not only that coins with obverses at this stage of development have an average weight of 90 grains, but that their reverses have a horse quite respectably portrayed, not the disjointed beast that appears on no. 1 and the generality of the Gaulish coins of the Atrebates and Morini. They are, in fact, unquestionably British coins, and exhibit distinct signs of improvement on the reverse, and the beginning of the same on the obverse.

Along with these go pieces like no. 6 (Evans, B. 9), with weights ranging from 94 to 83 grains, on which the head has obviously reached the same stage as no. 2. These coins, however, all bear the horse with triple tail and a wheel below the body of the horse, and so serve to mark the appearance of this peculiar tail as nearly contemporaneous with other types found in the Whaddon Chase hoard. This type (B. 9) was assigned by Evans to his Central district wherein the Whaddon

---

[1] *Rev. Num. Belge,* 1864, p. 430, pl. XXI.

Chase hoard came to light, and thus to the region which I
have credited with the introduction and development
of other new ideas in Celtic art. It may, I feel, be fairly
assumed that during the early period of the Catuvellaunian kingdom a coinage based on a stater of 90 grains
was in circulation, and that already this kingdom was
exercising considerable influence on its neighbours,
outvying them in wealth and power.

As already noted, it is now held that few British coins
antedate the second half of the first century B.C., and it
is further admitted that the coins of Commius (if the
attribution to Caesar's ally and ultimate foe is correct)
must date little if anything later than 50 B.C. His coin
(no. 7) and indeed that also of his son Tincommius
(no. 10) have obverses like that of the Whaddon Chase
type (B. 9), but they have both fallen in weight to about
83 grains (an 85-grain unit?). Their horse is still, however, a similar triple-tailed beast. After this issue Tincommius deserts this type entirely, and launches out
into others that suggest employment of foreign artists
using Roman republican and other such models. The
weight of their coins seems to represent the new standard
of about 85 grains coming into general use, since it is
that of the Surrey coin (no. 8) with obverse closely
resembling no. 4, but with the cruciform idea advanced
yet farther by filling all the angles of the cross with
lock-tassels, and continues almost constant apparently
to the close of the British numismatic epoch. It is,
moreover, the standard of the whole western series
bearing the triple-tailed horse, namely, those of Boduoc,
Comux, the Catti, Vocorio, and Eisu, and even of Antedrigus at his best, though many of his coins fall sadly
short of this standard.

Here we may assume with every justification that this group of western issuers borrowed the type, nay even the very idea of coinage, from the powerful Belgic tribes farther east; for were they not the original issuers of 'talei ferrei'? But it is worth observing that their idea of an obverse is essentially of their own creation. From the meaningless jumble of the usual obverse they seem to have selected half of the laurel-wreath, together with the central spot (e.g. on no. 5) and linked them together by a stalk into a symbol, of whose meaning one can hardly conceive they themselves were aware, but which at any rate has some specific form. There can be little doubt what it is. Sir John Evans describes it briefly as 'an object like a fern leaf or spike of flowers', but this description tends to confuse the issue, since it is apt to lead away from his considered opinion of its nature. For, as he very rightly says, 'Whatever it was intended to represent, there is little doubt that it is the legitimate descendant of the wreath of Apollo upon the earlier uninscribed coins, though some of the links in the chain of successive copies of copies are still wanting'.

One reservation—possibly it existed even in Sir John's mind when he wrote—needs to be emphasized; not all the uninscribed coins are earlier. The coin from Mt. Batten (Evans, C. 4) stands in the same relation to this series of coins as, for example, the Stamford Hill mirror to its more splendid predecessors from the Midlands. It seems at first a strange inversion of the usual practice of Celtic ornament,[1] but again Sir John

---

[1] Mr. Collingwood has, however, pointed out to me that parallels to such inversion do recur in Celtic art and that there seems at times to be a tendency for stylized and scattered elements to reassemble into theriomorphic groupings. That is possibly so, but when one comes to analyse the examples that come to mind, they seem not to represent the

Evans was undoubtedly right, when in commenting on the ear of corn, as it appears on the coins of Epaticcus (pl. VIII. 12) and the numerous examples issued by Cunobeline with the same motive, he observes, 'I have no doubt that one of the principal reasons for its adoption, was the similarity of the ear of corn to the laurel wreath, which, under one form or another, was so persistent upon the British coins, long after all other traces of the head of Apollo on their prototype had disappeared'. But, as already stated, it is actually evolved from the laurel-wreath, not merely adopted, because the ear of corn appears first on coins of rulers, whose issues do not begin until about the turn of the Christian era, and bear reverse types far in advance of anything employed on the western series. However much, therefore, one may discount the backwardness of the more westerly tribes in matters numismatic, their amazing productions in other fields of art makes it impossible to believe that by the time the central district had attained to types like those of Cunobeline, the western rulers would not have designed something better than these pieces. Typologically they are certainly earlier, and there can be little doubt that chronologically they are the same.   If the comparison of the spray with the ear of corn is apt, it would mean a survival of the triple-

true workings of the early Celtic spirit, but rather a fall below the zero mark at various stages of its life-history. The bird's head on some of the early pieces shows the process at work in a decadent la Tène II style; such cases are the horse-head from Stanwick (*B.M. Guide (Iron Age)*, 141, fig. 159), the face-like treatment of scrolls on the Hook Norton derivative of the thistle-brooch (*Archaeologia*, lxxx. 39, fig. 2 a), the dragonesque brooch evolved from pure scrolls or the ox-head sometimes found on late second-century trumpet-brooches, and finally the zoomorphizing trait in a later phase known as the 'Ultimate la Tène' (see *infra*, p. 141).

tailed horse in western and south-western Britain long
after it had passed out of existence farther east.

Already in that quarter the doom of the Apollo-head
was sealed. The orderly arrangement of the cruciform
principle wins the day, and leads to some amazing
developments. Tasciovanus's mint-masters evolved
designs, which, as the diagram suffices to show (nos. 11,
12, 15–17) all hark back to a common origin. A label
for his name was obtained by spreading apart the two
crescents in the centre of such an obverse as that of the
Surrey piece (no. 8). His son, Cunobeline, simply dis-
cards them. By another road, for example the Æ coin
inscribed VER or VIR for Verulamium (no. 16), the horns
of the crescents are prolonged into curling tendrils;
these are omitted on Dubnovellaunus's coin (no. 20)
which otherwise closely follows this Verulam type, and
even the bar, surviving from the laurel-wreath, ultimately fades away into mere shadow-lines of the border
of the design on an otherwise perfectly plain obverse
(e.g. D. 10).

But more amazing than all is Cunobeline's ear of
corn, evolved from nothing more or less than one-half
of the Verulam design. It is absurd to seek its origin in
any hypothesis of imitation of some imported Meta-
pontine drachma of four hundred years earlier (coins of
Baetica would afford a more contemporary model, if
such were needed), and it is probably quite beside the
mark to base its origin on surmises about the wealth
of British corn-lands. It is, in short, an outstanding
example of a rare phenomenon in early Celtic art in
Britain, the evolution of a purely natural motive from a
design which had passed through two centuries at least
of stylization. The laurel-wreath has become an ear of

corn. To say that British artists carried out the transformation unaided from first to last would be claiming
too much. Perhaps, as in many of the silver and bronze
coins of Tasciovanus, Cunobeline, and others, foreign
workmen played an important role, but it remains
nevertheless a striking monument to the conservatism
of the British gold coinage to which I have already
alluded.

In another direction the influence exercised by the
rulers established at Verulam can be clearly traced. It
is well known that they met at first with considerable
opposition from the Trinobantes, a tribe occupying an
area comprising modern Essex and probably parts of
Suffolk, but that later this tribe fell beneath the domination of its more powerful neighbours, so much so that
Cunobeline eventually transferred his seat to Camulodunum, the modern Colchester. Already, however, in
the days of Tasciovanus the influence of the Belgic
Catuvellauni is observable in the coinage of the chieftain, Addedomaros, who seems to have been located in
this district; for not only does this ruler on his coinage
present a purely cruciform version of the Apollo-head
without any of the adjuncts in the angles that appear,
for example, on no. 4 (C. 9) or on no. 8, the Surrey
type (D. 7), but he also strikes out a new line in a six-
rayed, Catherine-wheel arrangement, possibly prompted
by the slightly curved rays of Tasciovanus's early issues.
It is interesting to note here one of the few instances
of the Celtic triplication employed on coins, another
example being that of the Icenian Antedrigus, which
would seem to be a blend of Addedomaros's venture with
the type (no. 22) adopted for a large part of the silver
Icenian issues, which were clearly based on the Tascio-

Rigon model (no. 15). The curious obverse (no. 18) that appears on some of Addedomaros's coins must be a freakish transmogrification of the obverse of the Verulam bronze coins which furnish the link to Cuno-beline's wheat-ear type.[1]

The final descent of the Apollo-head is best illustrated by the remainder of the Icenian types, in which every reminiscence of the laurel-wreath, so religiously con-served in some form or other on nearly all the specimens hitherto examined, now passes out of our ken. Save that the decoration of no. 23 and no. 25 is obviously closely related to the design of the silver coins (no. 22) it would be impossible to declare that the simple cross of dots (no. 27) was the lineal descendant of the Apollo-head.

Allied in time must stand no. 26, the one type of all the British issues that, with the curving arms of its cross and its trefoil centre, seems numismatically to reproduce the spirit of Celtic ornament as we know it elsewhere.

Were it not for the clear link between the obverses of these Icenian coins and those of Tasciovanus, one would be prone to place the last two examples earlier, for their reverses preserve the zigzagged exergual line of the early Atrebatic series coins (e.g. B. 1). But this feature is rather to be regarded as a hark-back, since on some of the silver issues bearing the obverse (no. 22) the horse has its mane represented by a double line of dots, evidently influenced by the spray which surmounts the horse on some of Cunobeline's wheat-ear series. We find it exaggerated into a band of dot-filled zigzags above the horse on the Icenian coins, a group which

---

[1] Epaticcus's coin with the ear of corn can only be regarded as a copy of the larger series thus decorated, minted for Cunobeline.

I believe to ring the last echo of the Philip stater in Britain.

The Icenian coins, in short, like the enamels of the Santon Downham hoard (p. 45, *supra*), seem to owe their inception to influences of every kind diffused from the important and active centres of Verulamium and Camolodunum.

Already attention has been drawn to the effects of the extension of Roman power in Gaul upon Celtic art in other fields. Those effects also find an echo in British numismatics from the time of Tasciovanus onwards. But, except for the few instances noted above, one of which at least may be borrowed rather from Gaulish coins than from Roman, loans from Roman coin-types on the gold issues are restricted to a more lively presentation of the horse and the addition of a rider brandishing a trumpet instead of the Roman spear.

It is only in the silver coins that the British rulers seem to have indulged in excursions on a large scale into the repertory of Roman numismatics. There is something indeed strange in Tasciovanus and his son Cunobeline portrayed as the emperor Augustus himself with merely the addition of a legend to mark the coins as their own. The numerous examples of deliberate imitation of Roman types must form part and parcel of the peaceful penetration which Rome exercised on Britain in the century between Caesar's two invasions and the final conquest under Claudius. But none the less remarkable is the contrast to these afforded by other coins, especially those with heads of a veritable Celtic ferocity on the obverse. Are these earlier attempts at portraiture, or do they point to a steady falling away from the models set by the Augustan types? It is difficult to judge, but it may well be that some reaction set in during the last days of British freedom, and that these barbarous, uncouth heads illustrate the antagonism to Rome and all its works that Suetonius suggests in his description of Britain as *tumultuantem ob non redditos transfugas*.

Mr. Bushe-Fox in his report on Swarling rightly draws attention to the fact that it is dangerous to arrange the uninscribed coins in chronological order based on degradation of type or fall in weight, as these two factors do not by any means go together. This is certainly correct if one lumps the whole of the uninscribed coins together or attempts an arrangement on that basis alone. Obviously they cannot be dissociated from the earlier examples of the inscribed series. The very shortness of the life of the British coinage makes it essential to keep them together, the more so when it is remembered how soon, possibly within fifty years at most from the time the first coins were struck in Britain, rulers like Taciovanus were alloying their coinage with extensive loans of foreign motives.

The best results are to be obtained from a regional consideration of the earlier classes, or more strictly speaking, the classes based on the Philippic stater. The clearest demonstration is the series based on the Atrebatic and Morinic types in Evans's Central district.[1]

[1] The term Central is somewhat misleading. The actual focus of the Midlands lies in the Warwickshire plain, a region apparently almost unaffected by the early Iron Age, the range of which, as has been frequently demonstrated in recent years, is restricted to Dr. Cyril Fox's Lowland Zone, delimited by the line of the Jurassic Ridge from the Severn's mouth to Yorkshire. Beyond this the Iron Age culture in its early stages hardly penetrates at all, and except for a few discovered in South Wales, and some Brigantian specimens in south-west Yorkshire, British coins are scarcely ever discovered within his Palaeozoic boundary. Given this reduction of the early Iron Age sphere, the focus of the Central area naturally shifts south-eastwards to Hertfordshire and the Thames.

Here, as indicated above, the gradual transformation (it is only nominally degradation in this case) goes hand in hand with a fall in weight until a standard of 83 to 85 grains was reached.

The area of coinage so affected embraces the whole of south-east England, East Anglia, the upper Thames region, and that of the lower Severn and Somerset. Outside this we find two areas which seem to stand alone. The first is that assigned to the Brigantes, roughly speaking Lincolnshire, Yorkshire, and Nottinghamshire. The coins of this area were regarded by Sir John Evans as the latest of the British series. This conclusion can hardly be accepted. They are in point of fact a local development of the Atrebatic series, somewhat later than the Central group, because, though not differing in weight from the prototypes of that group, they start from a continental variation which has reached a more advanced stage of dissolution, marked by the reduction of the leaves of the laurel-wreath to mere billets.[1] There are some grounds for grouping these coins independently and for ascribing their origins to a separate settlement of Gaulish immigrants, moving up the East Coast and entering by the Wash and the Humber, in short, by the same road along which in my earlier pages I have ventured to suggest a special group of objects found their way northwards. The series, however, conforms to the general reduction of weight which the Central group underwent, and argues therefore for common economic conditions.

It was another group, however, that called forth

[1] This feature occurs on the Gallo-Belgic pieces called 'monnaies à l'epsilon' (*Rev. Num. Belge*, 1864, pl. XXI). They are considered (p. 430) to have been struck by people akin to and more or less adjacent to the Atrebates.

Mr. Bushe-Fox's observations, namely, that usually known as the South-western group. Here, again, the connotation of the title is not so clear as could be desired, since it does not include coins of the Comux-Antedrigus group, the distribution of which in Somerset and adjoining counties might naturally bring them under a similar heading. Actually the South-western group appears to have been centred in Hampshire, Wiltshire, and Dorset. Southern, pure and simple, would appear to be a better title. Artistically these coins stand in certain respects at the bottom of the ladder of numismatic art in Britain. The remains of the head on the obverse are, it is true, not greatly inferior to examples on other Atrebatic derivatives, but the reverse, even on the gold coins, is almost the last word (copper coins of the Hengistbury class are its final utterance) in the unintelligent imitation of the horse. Yet in spite of this degradation the standard of weight of the gold coins remains as high as 95 grains, and in some cases amounts to 100 or even 102 grains.

From their distribution one would be tempted to bring them into line with the Second Belgic invasion, which is deemed to have affected this region in particular.[1]

---

[1] I feel that in their recent controversy Messrs. Hawkes and Dunning have made out a strong case for their thesis on other grounds, and in that case the weight of these coins would represent a continuation of a continental standard by an entirely fresh group of immigrants. Unfortunately there is every reason to believe that the continental standard was falling even at the time of Caesar's conquest, and it was hardly likely to have been raised after its transference to Britain. Strangely enough these coins belong to an area which, in spite of the profusion of Iron Age camps indicating an extraordinary Celtic activity, figures far from prominently in the list of examples of Celtic art. It almost appears as if this area was too engrossed in military affairs to concentrate on the more settled life in which the peaceful arts could flourish.

An interesting commentary on their distribution is afforded by the two extreme limits of their occurrence. The one is the hoard found enclosed in a flint nodule at Westerham, on the western boundary of Surrey[1] and on the line of the prehistoric trackway, which in medieval times was famous as the Pilgrim's Way ; the other, the group of coins discovered at Karn Bré, near Camborne, Cornwall.[2] Examination of two coins from this latter site, now in the collections of the University of Oxford, has resulted in the discovery that they both come from dies employed to strike some of the coins in the Westerham hoard.

We can merely assume that they are an early issue in a region which for some reason unknown to us remained to the end unaffected by the artistic and economic changes which were taking place among its neighbours.

[1] *Num. Chron.*, 1927, p. 370, pls. XVI–XVII.
[2] W. Borlase, *Antiquities of Cornwall*, pl. XXIII, nos. X–XI.

IV

THE CELTS AS DELINEATORS OF HUMAN AND ANIMAL FIGURES AND AS PLASTIC ARTISTS

BRILLIANT though the success attained by the Celts in Britain was at the various zeniths of their artistic production, for there are two such points at least in their history, it must be conceded nevertheless that it was the result of a long process of development of motives borrowed in the first instance from classical sources. The achievements among continental Celts prior to the la Tène period are to say the best of them somewhat uninspiring and arid. Theirs was clearly no inherent creative genius such as that displayed by their Mediterranean contemporaries. They were clever copyists and adapters, and given the necessary impulses were certainly capable of arriving at an amazing sense of line in the realm of applied ornament. But at that point they stop. Nature, it seems, was to them almost a closed book. Throughout their artistic history it is impossible to detect those natural powers of accurate observation, the lack of which must constitute an eternal bar to entry into the higher spheres of art, among which plastic art takes a leading place. Their treatment of the classical palmette proves that they were endowed with little appreciation of the natural world in which they moved, for they added nothing fresh; they, like most of the peoples north of the Alps, exhibited an almost complete incapacity for any higher flights than linear ornament. Such attempts as they made are stamped in every case with the measure of their own limitations. It is not that they failed entirely, but that their efforts were bound in the very nature of things to result in what must be admitted is very poor success.

Nevertheless they made the attempt, and no account of their art would be complete without a short survey of their incursions into fields in which, unsupported by natural aptitude, they could hardly hope to succeed, namely, representation of human and animal forms.

Human form. In the portrayal of this, the most difficult subject to which any tiro can set his hand, they were doomed to failure from the first. Even their continental contemporaries fared little better, though they were nearer to the sources from which their models were derived. It needs only a glance at the coinage of Gaul to understand how unnatural it was for the Celt to go to nature itself for his inspiration. The whole history of that coinage is one of progressive copying, marked by diminishing intelligence the further in time and space the artists found themselves removed from the models on which that coinage was originally based.

'Understandest thou what thou readest?' said Philip to the Ethiopian. With the latter the Celts could truly have answered that they did not; but they had no Philip to set their feet in the way of understanding. So from the stater of Philip II of Macedon, a masterpiece of its period of Greek numismatic art, we can trace a history of imitation covering some three and a half centuries or more,[1] during which the fine lineaments of Apollo's face disappear into the limbo of oblivion, in which everything is sacrificed to an exaggeration of the

[1] Dr. Brooke has recently suggested that the beginnings of this imitative coinage in Gaul have been set too far back, and that in reality it dates from two important victories in Greece in the second century B.C., when immense booty of Philippic staters was poured into Rome to be adopted as a gold coinage for the Republic.

details of the hair and the laurel-wreath, until these in their turn fade away from all remembrance into meaningless rows of dots on the barbarous bronze coinage of southern Britain, best illustrated by the hoard discovered at Hengistbury Head, Hampshire, by Bushe-Fox in 1911.

It would not, however, be fair to suggest that the British Celts failed entirely. In the foregoing series they stood at the end of the road, at such distance that it was impossible to retrace their steps; but given a new path along which to tread, there might exist a reasonable hope that they could at least do no worse than their forebears in Gaul. The lively intercourse with Mediterranean lands in the century before the Claudian conquest brought them new models in coins from the late Republican and early Imperial mints, and with these to their hand the rulers of Britain essayed a coinage of their own. On some of the best efforts we can detect a conscious imitation of heads bound with a fillet, such as appear on the coins of the Roman gentes;[1] others (e.g. Tasciovanus) with unconscious flattery represented themselves as Augustus.[2] Cunobeline, too, appears less successfully as Augustus.[3] But side by side with these are others on which the Roman model is still recognizable, but the die-maker seems to present his chief as he was, or at least appears to attempt that task. In place of a beardless, fine-featured face and straight hair, taken from the Roman coin, we have a visage with high cheek-bones and beetling eyebrows, and the thick, curling hair of the Capitoline statue of the Dying Gaul, but unlike it with a thick beard in

[1] Eppillus, Evans, pls. III. 7, and XX. 2 and 5.
[2] Ibid., pl. XXI. 3, or possibly Antony, pl. XXI. 4 and pl. XXI. 11.
[3] Ibid., pl. XXII. 10.

addition to the moustache. So long, however, as it is a case of copying the portrait on the coin, it is often close enough to enable us to recognize the original. When the die-cutter attempts something on his own his result lacks all conviction. It is crude and puerile, a mere essay by one to whom portraiture was a magical but unfamiliar art.

It is the same childishness that marks endeavours to portray the human face for other purposes. The examples preserved to us are very few; if they have a merit, it is that they do present a type which corresponds closely to the Celt as we know him from the work of classical artists. But here we must again distinguish between foreign and native British work. I have already given reasons for assigning the Aylesford bucket to a continental workshop; to these may be added the smooth-faced head supporting the handle. It is as Celtic as the other work, but it is foreign. There is no parallel to it even on the British coins or elsewhere in these islands. The heads on the Marlborough bucket[1] come nearer to British work, but the long curling lock behind the head is a commonplace on Gaulish coins, and has no counterpart in this country.

It is otherwise with the bronze masks from Welwyn, Hertfordshire;[2] these are the acme of *naïveté*, with their wooden features and their staring eyes, an effect heightened by their lentoid frame, and with these go others from Peterborough, Northamptonshire,[3] where the eyes are delineated in the same childish manner.

Animal figures. Here as among most primitive peoples

[1] Sir R. Colt-Hoare, *Ancient Wilts*, ii. 33, pl. VI.
[2] *Archaeologia*, lxiii, pl. II.
[3] *Journal Brit. Arch. Ass.*, 1899, p. 61, pl. VII.

the Celts attained a greater measure of success, though, as is well known from their coinage, they were liable to fall away in the same manner as in their endeavours to produce the human form. In part this, again, is due to the long process of decadence which the horseman on the reverse of the Philip stater suffered in its passage across Gaul.

The influx of models from Italian and south Gaulish sources afforded, as in the case of the human heads, an opportunity for making, as it were, a new start; and thus in the period before the Roman conquest the work of the die-engravers shows a great improvement in the portrayal of the horse, as also of other animals, boar, hippocamp, pegasus, and eagle, employed on the reverses of coins struck in the south-eastern counties and in the district ruled by Tasciovanus and his successors north of the Thames. The Augustan types with capricorn and pegasus then became the models for fresh ventures, and these, together with the horseman and the riderless horse, are found associated with obverses on which the classical head is replaced by others with a Celtic physiognomy. Cunobeline, however, uses the same types and others with more marked success, so that it is perhaps difficult to assume an interval of manifest decadence between his coins and those of his father, though it is from Augustan coins that Tasciovanus must have taken the pegasus.

The coins of Tincommius, Verica, and Eppillus, who ruled in south-east Britain, display the same recourse to Roman types, and as a whole with greater exactitude in their imitative results. In point of style most of their coins stand alongside those of Cunobeline, but some struck for Tincommius occupy a position akin to the

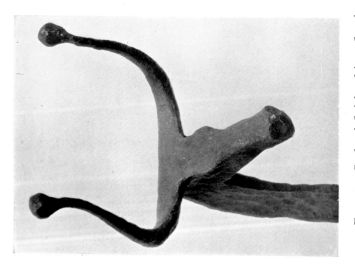

FIG. 27. Ox-head finials of iron fire-dog from Lord's Bridge, Cambs. Museum of Archaeology and Ethnology, Cambridge.

earlier examples of Tasciovanus. Some better success
was attained in the representation of animal figures in
the round. The heads of oxen added as finials to the
posts of iron firedogs of the late first century B.C. and
of the early part of the succeeding century are for the
most part crude and schematic, but in such cases as
those from Lord's Bridge, Barton, Cambridgeshire
(fig. 27),[1] we are conscious of a feeling for plastic art that
must have been indeed strong for the craftsman to have
beaten out of heated metal a work so lively and so
vigorous in its execution. The heads on the firedog
from Mt. Bures, Essex,[2] come near to equal success,
but in the examples[3] from Stanfordbury, Bedfordshire,
the treatment is stilted and formal, while the Welwyn[4]
heads have descended to mere smithery. But even if
these last are more sophisticated in character, they are
nevertheless of excellent workmanship; the twisted bars
welded to the amphora-stand found in the same tomb
(now exhibited in model in the British Museum and
illustrated on the same plate as the firedog) witness to
a very high degree of technical skill.

All the above-mentioned examples come from the
eastern counties. The only other analogous specimens,
two in number, at present known curiously enough
come from Wales and its border. Two similar heads on
a smaller scale from Lydney, Gloucestershire[5] (they
measure no more than 3 inches high), are attached to a

[1] *Ant. Journ.* vi. 316, figs. 1–3.
[2] *Arch. Cambrensis*, 1912, p. 103, fig. 31.
[3] C. Fox, *Arch. Camb. Region*, pl. XVII.
[4] *B.M. Guide (Iron Age)*, pl. XII.
[5] *Reports of the Research Committee of the Society of Antiquaries of London*, No. IX; R. E. M. Wheeler and T. V. Wheeler, *Excavation of the prehistoric, Roman, and post-Roman Site in Lydney Park, Gloucestershire*, p. 74, fig. 11, no. 9.

fragment of an iron vessel, possibly part of a tripod not unlike those of Greek or Italo-Greek origin found in the Rhineland and France. The heads are in this instance admirably executed, and rank beside those from Lord's Bridge. It is otherwise with those on the firedogs from Capel Garmon, Denbighshire.[1] These lack the quality of either the Lydney examples or of those from Lord's Bridge or from Mt. Bures, and the rest of the work on the dogs is overloaded and fantastic.

In bronze a few somewhat stylized productions are known. The first is on a handle found in association with the Birdlip mirror,[2] and demonstrates by mere contrast with the superb craftsmanship of the mirror itself the shortcomings of the Celt in his observation of natural forms. The second, from Ham Hill, Somerset,[3] is much better, though the treatment of the muzzle shows the Celt subservient to his ineradicable attraction towards a curvilinear style; the nostrils are represented by coiled mouldings, and the eyes are outlined, as in the Welwyn human masks, by a lentoid frame. If it is to be dated by the associated coins to the fourth century, a head from Parc y Meirch Wood, Kinmel Park, Dinorben, Flintshire,[4] proves that the Celt practically never freed himself from this attraction. It is, however, probably earlier, as it presents considerable affinities, especially in the treatment of the muzzle, to the example from Lydney noted below. Mouldings of a similar character, for example, are employed on a mount from Aldborough, Yorkshire.[5]

[1] *Arch. Cambrensis*, 1912, p. 102, fig. 30.
[2] *Archaeologia*, lxi. 332, fig. 2.
[3] *Proc. Soc. Ant.* xxi. 133.
[4] *Arch. Cambrensis*, 1913, p. 195, fig. 2.
[5] R. G. Collingwood, *Roman Britain* (1923), p. 9 and fig.

FIG. 28. Enamelled bronze handle from Harpenden, Herts. ($\frac{1}{1}$). (Luton Museum).

How far beneath the Lydney iron heads stands
another in bronze from the same site,[1] forming part
of an attachment of unknown purpose! The nature of
the animal with its down-curving horns is unmistakable, and yet the work is poor in the extreme, entirely
lacking the vigour of the iron pieces. The contrast in
quality corresponds to the difference in date. The iron
heads are products of the excellent period of Celtic art
in Britain a little before or after the Christian era. The
bronze specimen bears the hall-mark of a later date, not
only in the triangular arrangement of the fields for the
enamel (see p. 112), but also in the presence of two
colours, red and green.[2] The colour is stated by the
authors of the report to be green, but I suspect rather
that it should be light blue, possibly of a greenish tinge.
The presence of green enamel would place the piece well
within the Roman period, not earlier than the second
century, but the style is that of a whole group of horse-
trappings and the like which, as we shall see, are in
evidence at the time of the conquest. The treatment of
the ox-head is simply puerile, but it is Celtic, and Celtic
art on the down-grade.

No sharper contrast to this feeble production could
be desired than the two massive bronze handles found
in association with turned wooden vessels at Harpenden,
Hertfordshire (fig. 28).[3] The staples are cast in the form
of an animal's head. They are stated in the original
account to be in that of a horse. This is incorrect, for the
transversely ribbed, curling horns, the large, full lips,
and the nostrils set high on the muzzle stamp it at once
as that of a ram, and a very masterly representation it is.

---

[1] Op. cit., fig. 11, no. 12.   [2] See note on p. 98.
[3] *Ant. Journ.* viii. 520, pls. LXXXII and LXXXIII.

In their original condition the staples must have lent great distinction to the vessel they served to adorn. The long, narrow face with massive horns was rendered even more forceful by the insertion of bosses of red enamel in the expanded nostrils, while others of smaller size (now lost) set within narrow lids added to the hot fierceness of a lean, old, fighting pasha of the flock. The significance of similar bosses of red enamel in a large, cupped depression on each side of the mouth (now also wanting) is not so clear, but must have heightened the general effect produced by the other bosses of the same material. Mr. Reginald Smith has very rightly assigned these handles to the early part of the first century B.C.; they cannot be later. They belong, in short, to the apogee of Celtic art before its gradual wane in the succeeding decades. It may here be noted that the ram is rare in British Celtic art, but is known on firedogs on the Continent, for example at Arras, France.[1]

The few examples of minor statuary in bronze reveal the usual failings. A small bull, from an unknown site, but unquestionably belonging to this general period (formerly in the collection of the Rev. James Douglas and given by Sir Richard Colt-Hoare to the Ashmolean Museum in 1834), is a poor creature with a hollow back and weak knees that does little credit to the artist (fig. 29 c). For the height of Celtic absurdity in this field nothing could perhaps surpass the animal-finials from Belbury Camp, Dorset.[2]

Favourite with the Celts alike on the Continent and in the British Isles, as proved by its frequent appearance on the coinage, as also on such pieces as the shield from the river Witham, is the boar. That on the Witham shield

---

[1] *Archaeologia*, lxiii. 6, fig. 9.   [2] Ibid. xlviii. 115, pl. VI. 1–2.

a *b*

c

FIG. 29. (*a*) Jet pendant with Medusa-head from Rochester, Kent ($\frac{1}{1}$). Ashmolean Museum. (*b*) Bronze mask from Charterhouse-on-Mendip, Somerset ($\frac{2}{3}$). Copyright of the Bristol Museum and Art Gallery. Bristol Museum. (*c*) Bronze ox, locality unknown ($\frac{1}{1}$). Ashmolean Museum.

shows by its ludicrously attenuated legs how little stress the Celt placed on anything resembling exact representation even for a purpose of so heraldic a character. In the round we find the same weakness as in the bulls; the animal is at best a very sorry hog. So it is with the two larger examples from Hounslow, Middlesex,[1] in the British Museum; a third of smaller size is animated with rather more spirit. An imperfect boar from Guilden Morden, Surrey,[2] is a crude thing. The best in many respects for all its childish exaggeration is the pert little beast from Woodendean, Sussex.[3] The Hounslow boars were associated with two other animals, on the nature of which it is difficult to decide; one may be a horse, the other a dog or wolf, but neither carries much conviction.

To a time just before the coming of Rome belongs a small group of brooches in bronze with repoussé disks on a circular back-plate. All are ornamented with animal figures. One from Westhall, Suffolk,[4] formed part of the large hoard of horse-trappings and other objects from that site. The nature of the animal is difficult to recognize; it is possibly meant for a wolf, though it has some of the characters of the horse as portrayed on some of the British coins. Rather more certain is a second example from Santon Downham, Suffolk,[5] also from the hoard found there. Here we seem to have a British conception of the griffin. But there is absolutely no question about a third from Lancing, Sussex. This is an unmistakable hippocamp (fig. 30 a).[6]

[1] B.M. Guide (Iron Age), 147, fig. 172.
[2] Cambs. Ant. Soc., Reports and Comm. x. 373.
[3] Proc. Soc. Ant. xxi. 489.
[4] Archaeologia, xxxvi. 455, pl. xxxviii. 5.
[5] Cambs. Ant. Soc. Reports and Comm. xiii. 154, fig. 7.
[6] Gentleman's Magazine, 1830, July, p. 17, pl. ii. 13.

In all cases the animals must have been borrowed from the same sources as supplied the models for the Romanizing coin-types of Tasciovanus, Cunobeline, and other rulers. The figures are simple enough, but are well placed upon the roundel and give the impression of execution by workmen acquainted with some of the niceties of medallic art. All three are in the same style, and their associations with other objects and their stylistic analogies to the fabulous animals introduced on to the copper and silver coinage serve alike to assign them to the early part of the first century A.D.

Roman period. The efforts of the Celt in the same fields during the Roman occupation call for only a short account and may for convenience be included in the present chapter.

We have seen how quickly the Celt in pre-Roman days fell away from the models provided for him by Roman coins. It is therefore not surprising to find that even under Roman rule he was still unable to profit to any great extent by the rich material for study in the shape of figurines and statuary which were imported during the Roman occupation. In fact, he shows little endeavour to make use of the opportunities thus afforded him, and at almost every turn we are confronted by a persistence of the same incapacity to reproduce either the human or animal forms.

Here and there in England, as on the Continent, we meet with flat pendants of Whitby jet on which is carved a Medusa's head. Their place of manufacture is vouched for by examples in the York Museum, only one of the numerous uses to which the material was put, among the rich collections of jet objects in that museum. They must have been carried over to the Continent more as

a   b

c   d

FIG. 30. (*a–b*) Bronze brooch and nielloed bronze pendant from Lancing, Sussex. (*c*) Bronze dragonesque fibula from Suffolk. (*d*) Bronze trumpet fibula from (?) N. Ireland. All Ashmolean Museum ($\frac{1}{1}$).

curiosities or souvenirs than as amulets with efficient apotropaic powers. For the stringy hair and mild-eyed, narrow faces are the very acme of feebleness contrasted with the curling, snaky locks and terrifying lineaments of the classical type. It would almost be difficult, apart from the place of manufacture, to imagine that they were the work of either Roman or Celt, but that some are probably that of Romanized natives seems indicated by the remarkable specimen (fig. 29 *a*) from the vicinity of Rochester published by Sir Arthur Evans,[1] interesting because the head is depicted in profile and is manifestly a Celtic type with thick masses of hair, while the snakes are introduced as mere adjuncts into the field of the pendant, and are not shown entwined in the hair itself.

The feebleness that stamps such works as these repeats itself in the bronze mask from Charterhouse-on-Mendip, Somerset (fig. 29 *b*).[2] The soft curves of the cheeks, the childish moulding of the mouth, the exaggeration of the eye-sockets, and the curious treatment of the hair, all serve to stamp the mask as a native effort to imitate a classical style.

But once at least the Celt may be said to have succeeded to the full. Trained perhaps in some Roman sculptor's workshop, but endowed with a genius rare among his countrymen, a Celt, and as Professor Haverfield put it, a Celt alone, could have wrought into the features of the Gorgon's head, carved in stone, from Bath, a fierce, virile vigour that finds no kin in Greek or Roman art.

This is the most important work of a Celtic sculptor that has come down to us; other works that have to be

---

[1] *Archaeologia*, lxvi. 572, fig. 5.
[2] *V. C. H. Somerset*, i. 337, fig. 94.

placed to his credit have been fully appreciated in *The Romanization of Roman Britain*. Haverfield shows how the Celt, by that time with his eye better trained, was able to impart a vigorous treatment to the hunting scenes on the native-made Castor ware, but yet displays the same inability to depict the human form with any greater accuracy than before.

Note to p. 93

In anticipation of further remarks in Chapter V on the relationship between a particular phase of Celtic ornament and the triangular enamelled fields, I call attention here to the specially excellent illustration afforded by the little mount from Chepstow, Monmouthshire[1] (fig. 20 *b*). Its admirably designed S-scroll, recalling in the details of its treatment the Berkshire disk (fig. 21 *c*), is set between two plates decorated with a double band of triangles, alternately in red and yellow enamel. Here Celtic curves, as free as could well be desired, but with enamelled finials already displaying the incipient 'boss' style, are combined with a dry angular decoration (compare the Trelan Bahow mirror (fig. 19), a combination that, in spite of the frequent use of such angular patterns on pottery in western Britain, is the very antithesis of all that Celtic curvilinear ornament connotes, and one that as such—on bronze at any rate—seems previously to have been rigorously eschewed.

[1] *Arch. Cambrensis*, 1932, 393.

V

THE COMING OF ROME

ALREADY before the Claudian conquest we have ample evidence that the British were being drawn into the net of Mediterranean commercialism, which, starting long before with the trade set up by the Etruscans and by the Greek colonies of southern Gaul, by this time had fallen entirely into the hands of Rome and her subjects. Not only the graves of British chieftains in the eastern counties, as at Stanfordbury and Welwyn, have produced along with firedogs and other gear of their own native work products of Italian marts, silver goblets, bronze patellae, oenochoae, and the like, but even in their cities signs of the same contact with a wider world have come to light. As the excavators of Colchester have observed, Cunobeline was introducing his people to Arretine dinner-services. The Lexden tumulus outside Colchester contained bronze vessels and figurines of Italian workmanship.[1]

This trade was unfortunately already having a deleterious effect on Celtic art. Its boldness of phantasy, its strength, and its inventiveness were gradually being sapped by easy access to the products of the steadily increasing mass-production of the Roman Empire. Not every trace of Celtic feeling disappears, but the remnant left behind is harnessed to an obvious attraction to the cheap tawdriness that mass-production always brings in its train. We have few pieces with which to illustrate the initiation of the process, but happily they can be fairly closely dated.

Three of the legions which landed in Britain in A.D. 43

[1] *Archaeologia*, lxxvi. 241–54.

came from the Rhine, and one of them, the Second
Augusta, had previously been stationed at Mainz.
Under the command of Vespasian it was entrusted with
the reduction of southern Britain, and we know that it was
engaged in Dorset and Wiltshire in 43, that it had gained
command of the Mendip lead-mines by 45, and that it
was established at Caerleon before 75. At various points
which this legion may have reached, for example,
Lancing Down, Sussex (fig. 30 b), and notably the Celtic
hill-fort on Hod Hill, a little north-west of Blandford,
Dorset, trappings, buckles, and other gear in bronze
decorated with niello-work have come to light. These
are of Rhenish fabric and can by finds at Hofheim and
the Saalburg be closely dated between A.D. 40 and 80.
Clearly in a native hill-fort like Hod Hill their presence
is to be ascribed to the Roman legion. Celtic objects
have also been found there, but these must all be dated
before the Roman occupation of Dorset, since it was
notoriously part of Roman policy to drive the natives
from their hill-top strongholds down to the valleys.
An interesting commentary on this attribution is afforded
by the discoveries at Silchester in Reading Museum.
The town of Calleva Atrebatum, it is held, must have
been either founded, or, if a prior settlement existed
there, effectively organized by Commius, on whose
son's coins the name CALLEV appears.[1] But strangely
enough little with an early Celtic facies was recovered;
merely a few British coins and an enamelled cheek-
piece of a bridle-bit. In addition, however, to several
small penannular brooches, a well-known British form,

---

[1] Dr. Brooke doubts whether the distribution of Eppillus's coins
warrant the connexion of the inscription with Silchester; his seat of
government apparently lay farther east in Kent.

there is a small group of thistle-brooches, imported jewellery, but apparently fashionable among the native population before the conquest,[1] while, on the other hand, there is none of the Rhenish nielloed work. The town was evidently not occupied for any length of time by Roman forces; apparently it submitted quickly; after all Commius and his tribe had for a time been in league with the Romans. The nielloed work appears rather at more outlying points where resistance was stronger and where the activities of the legions were more pressingly engaged.

Among the Celtic things found on Hod Hill are tankard-handles in which the spirit of Celtic art is obviously in decline. They are but a poor shadow of the Trawsfynydd type. Some, like the piece illustrated in the *B.M. Guide* (*Iron Age*), fig. 146, still show the true Celtic feeling in its curves and mouldings,[2] others have the scrolls reduced to a series of slightly raised disks decorated with a boss encircled by an engraved line. The largest known group of such handles is that from a hoard found at Seven Sisters, near Neath, Glamorganshire, South Wales. They are associated with pieces of the same nielloed bronze, doubtless due to the proximity of the Roman forces in the West. Confirmation of the date of the tankard-handles ornamented in this manner is supplied by the Welwyn finds, among which was such a handle.[3] There can be no

----

[1] Evidence of this, already in part established by comparison of finds like Stanfordbury and Santon Downham, is steadily gaining corroboration from such sites as Colchester.

[2] The same double-linked grouping of curves round three large openings is repeated in a simpler manner on a plate from Stanwick (*Archaeologia*, lx. 289, fig. 35).

[3] *Archaeologia*, lxiii. 21, fig. 21.

question that the grave in which it was discovered was anterior to the conquest, or that it belonged to exactly that period during which intercourse with the Continent was particularly strong; that is, in the times of such rulers as Cunobeline, and thus to the early part of the first century. This small but useful piece of evidence permits us to group together the later enamels of the eastern class, the latest of the engraved mirrors, the firedogs with ox-head finials, and these tankard-handles. It is probable that in the Seven Sisters hoard they antedate to some degree the horse-trappings, but the Roman nielloed work may be almost contemporary, though of course imported later. In addition, at Seven Sisters we have other objects purely native in fabric, all of which serve to illustrate my point in regard to the decadence from which Celtic art was beginning to suffer.

The group of horse-trappings, in point of general form closely akin to some from Stanwick, North Yorkshire, while not entirely devoid of the Celtic spirit as shown by the treatment of S-shaped scrolled filling of one piece, a treatment which also occurs on a mount from Stanwick, exhibits in other respects a further stage of the downward path on which another set of trappings from Stanwick—to which belongs the ring (*B.M. Guide* (*Iron Age*), fig. 155) with its numerous niggling little dots of enamel[1] in place of the bold infrequent spots of the earlier work—has clearly set its foot. This latter Stanwick set includes a terret with flat-topped bosses arranged in pairs, a further development of the round-topped bosses on that from the Seven Sisters hoard. The Stanwick

---

[1] An alternative use of small spots, not in enamel, but in the form of small bosses, is to be seen on a fastening found at Lydney, Gloucestershire (R. E. M. and T. V. Wheeler, *Lydney*, fig. 11. 10).

II. LATER ENAMELS

1, Colchester, Essex ; 2, 4, 5, Seven Sisters, Glamorgan ;
3, Canterbury, Kent

Scale a little over one-half

terret, though decorated in an older tradition of red enamelled spots, must, however, on account of the disposition of its bosses in pairs, be regarded as later than the Seven Sisters piece.

The Seven Sisters hoard, however, has yielded evidence of a further step on the downward path in taking as its model the fashion of a certain class of provincial Roman fibulae ornamented with rectangular cells filled with enamel along the top of the bow; the trappings in that hoard have large portions of their outer surfaces covered with an alternation of red and yellow enamel in little cells (pl. II. 4, 5), producing a rather cheap, jewelled effect, a great falling away from the strong interplay of colour in the contrast of large, bold designs in red enamel against the yellow of the bronze itself.[1] The upper face of the terret knobs still follows the tradition of the lipped terrets of the Polden Hill hoard on which the enamel is so arranged as to form with the bronze a quatrefoil design (pl. I. 2), but here again the whole face of the knob is filled with enamel. This, as from now on becomes usual, is red and yellow (pl. II. 2), but, as shown by a terret from a hoard of closely analogous trappings found at Saham Toney, Norfolk, the colours can have blue also added.[2] This latter combination of colour seems to place the Saham Toney trappings on stylistic grounds a little later than those from Seven Sisters, an assumption which is borne out by other details of the hoard, even though there is no extraneous

---

[1] The process is well illustrated by a cheek-piece from Bower Chalke, Wilts., in which a succession of four blue and three red spots, four of them round, the others square, are used (*Wilts. Arch. Mag.* xliii. 352). It makes a poor showing beside the Polden Hill examples.

[2] *V. C. H., Norfolk,* i, pl. opp. p. 273, upper left.

material as at Seven Sisters by which to confirm it.[1]
At any rate on a terret from Saham Toney the effect of
jewelling comes out even more conspicuously. Here the
upper edge (for by this time some of the terrets have
their rings rectangular in section) has a line of cells
filled with an alternation of three colours, red, yellow,
and light blue, not the dark blue of the glass occasionally
used for spots in the earlier broad terrets from the east
of England. An even more striking example is a
terret in Colchester Museum,[2] which has not only
both faces decorated with squares in red and yellow,
but also its fore-edge with about a score of squares in
red, yellow, and blue (pl. II. 1). One may note in passing
that in the demands of this imitation of jewellery one
point was lost from view. In the older class of terrets
the enamel was placed in a position to catch the eye
from the ground, to impress the bystander watching a
chieftain hurtling past in his swiftly driven chariot.
In the later examples the requirements of the celled
effect caused the enamel usually to be set only along the
top, where it might be momentarily seen, as the
chariot passed by, but not while coming and going alike,
as would be possible with the lipped terrets. In every
respect the work of this period is of a flimsier character;
one suspects some economy of metal. Of the original
appearance of some of the Saham Toney pieces we can
never be absolutely sure, since the enamel is now lost,
but by analogy with contemporary pieces from other
sites it becomes certain that red and yellow were
the favourite and prevailing combination of colour.

[1] The elimination of blue in enamel-form at an earlier stage makes
it the more interesting to discover at what exact period the British
succeeded in adding it to their stock of enamel-colours.

[2] *Colchester Museum Report*, 1926, p. 25, no. 5233. 26.

The combination with light blue, however, occurs on another piece from Saham Toney, though the second colour has now entirely disappeared from the alternate cells.

In this class of cellular decorated work fall many of the semi-Celtic fibulae found on Roman sites in Britain; in style they are often based on imported forms, but the work is carried out with a solidity and strength which makes the imported specimens look mere gewgaws when placed beside them. One other object has to be included here, namely the sword from Embleton,[1] Cumberland. Its strap-band at the middle of the scabbard and chape alone would date it late; the latter is of the type which Déchelette assigned to his la Tène IV. Its decoration of little square cells of enamel in three colours, red, yellow, and blue, makes this dating even more certain.

Throughout the Roman occupation of Britain we witness a continuous struggle of the Celt to save his native decoration from the cold formalism of Roman art. Perhaps nowhere does this struggle make itself more felt, and the results appear more successful than in the series of fibulae which Roman sites have produced. For amid the multifarious types which are the common possession of the western provinces of the Empire, Britain can show others that are practically unknown on the Continent, and these we owe unquestionably to the Celtic element in the population. Most of these fibulae are adaptations of Roman provincial forms, but in all the Celt embellished the originals, bringing them into consonance with the urge of his unconquerable phantasy. It is not difficult to illustrate this point.

(1) One of the commonest fibulae on Roman sites in

[1] J. M. Kemble, *Horae Ferales*, 193, pl. XVIII. 3.

Britain is the so-called trumpet fibula (fig. 30 *d*), the history of which can be traced back through such types as that represented by the Aylesford fibula found in a cremation-grave of the first century B.C. Here the Celt, chiefly during the first half of the second century A.D., by borrowing the classical acanthus, in his own peculiar method and in accordance with his own peculiar feeling resuscitated what was originally quite a graceful, if simple form, from a state of dryness and commonplaceness to which it had degenerated in eastern France and western Germany during the first century. Or to put it in the words of Mr. Collingwood,[1] 'It is hardly too much to infer that the native craftsmen had learnt from the Romans a pattern which solved the decorative problem with which at the moment they were struggling, the problem of making the trumpet-brooch into a thing whose lines should flow gracefully into each other throughout its length'. But when Mr. Collingwood adds that 'the trumpet-brooch is no product of the unaided British imagination, but the fruit of a union between imported Roman ideas and native British workmanship', and that 'it arose only after the Roman conquest of the less Romanized part of Britain, and only as a result of the stimulus given by classical art, even in a debased and mechanical form, to the British artist's mind',[2] I feel that his words do not do full justice to the position. The term trumpet-brooch is a name which by courtesy, nothing else, has come to be applied to a Romano-British form. But the elements of the form, the swollen head, which give it its trumpet-like shape, go back to pre-Roman times. To the new form thus devised the Celt added little touches

---

[1] *Archaeologia*, lxxx. 47.   [2] Op. cit. 47–8.

FIG. 31. Set of bronze horse-trappings from Stanwick, Yorkshire ($\frac{1}{4}$).
British Museum.

of his own scroll-designs and frequently heightened these with enamel. During the first years of Roman conquest and occupation he had no time to evolve entirely fresh forms for himself; he had perforce to borrow from his new masters; and what he found to borrow were the miserably uninspiring shapes brought over from the continental factories. Within quite a short while by taking over, as was his invariable practice, just those motives that appealed to his fancy he had infused as it were a new vigour into a lifeless thing. If it is true that the Celtic mind was incapable of inventing its decorative motives unaided, it is even more applicable to other races. For when one examines Celtic art closely, one is amazed to find how small is the loan which it has sought from its neighbours and how high is the rate of interest which it pays.

Mr. Collingwood has shown that this process of adaptation can be observed in the western counties where certain varieties of the trumpet-brooch seem to have arisen, but that the finest examples of the process emanated from northern England. Further, he has maintained with some force that there seems to have existed a definitely northern British school which succeeded in keeping alive the Celtic spirit within the bounds of the Roman province. The group lies close to the Wall and marks an outlier of the Celtic world, cut off from the main body by the Wall itself.

(2) *The dragonesque fibula.* Its origin is obscure, but in my opinion the earlier form is nothing more than an S-shaped adaptation of scrolls derived from the broken-backed scroll of the pre-Roman period surviving into Roman times. The example from Lakenheath[1]

---

[1] *V.C.H., Suffolk*, i. 271, pl. opp. 272.

(fig. 30 c) shows the Celt a master of his own craft, but the jewel-like decoration of Roman fibulae caught his wayward fancy, and the flat S-brooch with enamel is the result. It is only in the later examples, and those principally from the north, that the addition of eyes and the lifting of the ends of the scrolls into ear-like appendages transformed the fibula to its more realistic dragonesque appearance.

Thus we find the Celtic invention copied in a simple, flat form at Braughing, Hertfordshire,[1] a site which produced several objects little, if at all, later than the Claudian invasion. In this specimen the curves of the middle section closely follow those of the Lakenheath brooch. One point has to be kept in mind. By A.D. 100 there was little or no true Celtic work, such as the Lakenheath fibula undoubtedly is, being made in southeast Britain. Collingwood places the beginning of the eye at about that date and its full development before 130 to 140. The eyeless variety therefore falls typologically before 100, and if that be so, it is the unmistakably Celtic example which must be regarded as representative of the ancestry of the whole series. Those without eyes do occur in the south, but even their greater frequency in the north may well be due to a tendency, wholly natural and easily explicable, for objects, even though of Roman form, but altered in accordance with native taste, to appear on the periphery of the part of Britain already subjugated by Rome. It is shortly before the building of Hadrian's Wall that the decadence of Celtic work south of the Wall becomes most marked. The Romanization of Roman Britain was approaching its zenith.

[1] *Archaeologia*, lxxx. 53, fig. 11 a.

Pieces like the Aesica fibula (fig. 20 *c*) are valuable as demonstrating how very alive the Celtic spirit still remained in the latter part of the first century, for not only do I agree with Collingwood that this fibula can be dated as early as 100, but am even of opinion that it can be placed still earlier. Collingwood's examination of the evidence on this point is well worthy of the most serious consideration.

Later the Celtic spirit lost its strength south of the Wall, but I must entirely disagree with Collingwood when he says that the people who made the brooches, which we have seen to be a blend of Roman and Celtic, 'owed to the new Roman influence much of what made their work art instead of mere craft'. The exact converse seems to approach more nearly to the truth. Without the feeling for the grace of curving line, which is so brilliantly represented by one of the sets of Stanwick harness (fig. 31),[1] hardly deserving the stigma of a somewhat effete and formalized decoration, which Mr. Collingwood, perhaps influenced by other constituents of the hoard, attaches to the Stanwick school, the provincial Roman fibula in Britain would have remained the dry, unimaginative thing that most of its continental contemporaries undoubtedly are. It is because the Stanwick hoard contains pieces which bear the taint of the new continental influences that some of them fall short of the vigour and taste which stamps what were their predecessors in the south, not, as Mr. Collingwood imagines, contemporaries. What might have been effected if the school, if school it is, had been left undisturbed, the fine set of trappings mentioned above more than amply proves. At an earlier stage

[1] To this set belongs *B.M. Guide* (*Iron Age*), fig. 156.

attention has been drawn to the tendency towards the bizarre which began to infect Celtic art just before the coming of Rome with its formalizing influences, and wherever the art still managed to assert itself it is thenceforward never quite free from that tendency. Even on so fine a thing as the torc from Lochar Moss the trait is plain, but there are other pieces, for the most part not far removed in time from that of the torc, which exhibit the same trait in a more marked degree. We may begin with a small embossed plate, part of a hinged fastening, found in a comparatively early association in Thirst House Cave, Derbyshire.[1] Its decoration consists of the broken-backed scroll arranged in a fantastic fashion which resembles some pseudo-calligrapher's florid conception of the letter N. On the armlet from Plunton Castle, Kirkcudbrightshire (fig. 32 f),[2] where it has a disjointed look, and on the torc from Stichel, Roxburghshire,[3] where the fantasy of the draughtsman has gone to greater lengths, the idea is clearly in close touch with the 'boss' style, which comes so markedly into evidence in the north from the close of the first century (fig. 32). A fair idea of the date of this curious motive is afforded by its employment on a seal-box of Roman form from Lincoln, enamelled in red and blue,[4] and another of similar character in Liverpool Museum.[5]

The infection of native work under Roman rule makes itself still more evident towards the close of the first century and onwards. The enamel cell-work up to this

---

[1] *V.C.H., Derby*, i. 233, fig. 35.
[2] *Cat. Nat. Mus. Scottish Ant.* 200, FA 36.
[3] Daniel Wilson, *Archaeology and Prehistoric Annals of Scotland*, 451; *Cat. Nat. Mus. Scottish Ant.* 200, FA 37.
[4] *B.M. Guide to the Antiquities of Roman Britain*, fig. 117.
[5] Mayer Collection 9614.

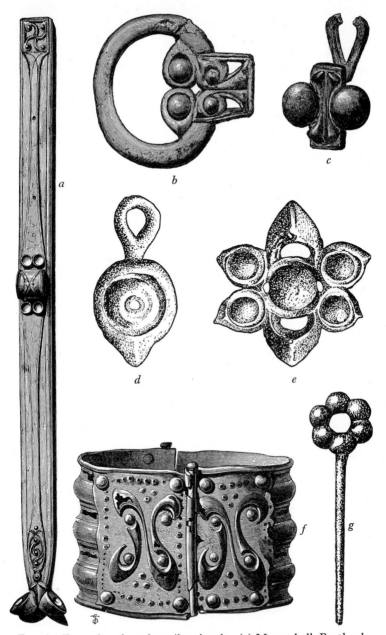

FIG. 32. Examples of northern 'boss' style. (*a*) Mortonhall, Pentland;
(*b*) Stanhope, Peeblesshire; (*c*) Lochspouts crannog, Maybole, Ayrshire;
(*d*, *e*, and *g*) Traprain Law, Haddingtonshire; (*f*) Plunton Castle,
Kirkcudbrightshire.

point generally arranged in squares is supplemented
by others in triangles and lozenges, for the former of
which the Saham Toney ring of a bridle-bit furnishes
a good example.[1] Triangles arranged in lozenges also
appear on another piece from the same hoard,[2] a harness-
fitting of quatrefoil form with light-blue enamel (possibly
glass) laid on with such an economy of preparatory
chasing of the metal and with so thin a flux of colour
that it resembles rather a mere coat of paint than the
thick enamelling of pre-Roman days; if really enamel,
it is probably one of the earliest examples of the use of
blue by a British craftsman that we possess. This piece
is of further interest in that the sides of two of the leaves
of the so-called quatrefoil increase in size and thickness
until they meet in a median ridge and run out to a point.
Here we have the trumpet-motive transferred from
flat enamel-work to a solid casting other than those of
fibulae, or it may be a development of the moulding at
the base of objects like the Birdlip mirror and round the
Moel Hiraddug plate. The effect in combination with
enamel is excellently illustrated by the bridle-bit from
Rise, near Hull. This bit also retains the enamelled
quatrefoil in a roundel of the Seven Sisters and Saham
Toney terrets, but has in addition small square studs
similarly decorated at the middle of each side of the
rings. A fragment of such a ring occurred at Traprain
Law,[3] Haddingtonshire, so that, as will be seen later,
the Rise bit does not follow the Saham Toney trappings
immediately, but is separated from them probably by
an interval of a half century or more, and is probably to
be dated to the early second century.

---

[1] *V. C. H. Norfolk*, i, pl. opp. p. 273, right lower.
[2] Ibid. centre.   [3] *Proc. Soc. Ant. Scot.* lvi. 258, fig. 24. 3.

A few words may here be inserted about Celtic horse-furniture. One of the most widely employed objects for purposes of dating in prehistoric and, leaving aside coins, in protohistoric times is unquestionably the fibula, and its value is fully recognized in British archaeology. The mere mention of horse-trappings is liable to arouse derision; they are too apt to be regarded as the last resource of the despairing archaeologist, at a loss to account for the purpose of a particular object. But unquestionably the horse-trappings of the period under review, from their first appearance down to the third century of our era, are of first-class importance as material for dating. They form so rich a series among British remains, and keep such close step with the changes in decorative style observable on other classes of objects, that they can be employed as criteria for relative chronology with almost the same confidence as other things upon which reliance is more normally placed. The two parts of harness which are most characteristic for this purpose are the bridle-bit and the terret-ring.

The bridle-bit. (*a*) The earliest is that represented by finds at Hagbourne Hill, Berkshire;[1] Hunsbury, Northamptonshire;[2] Ulceby, Lincolnshire;[3] and at Hunmanby[4] and in the King's Barrow at Arras in the East Riding of Yorkshire.[5] It is a snaffle-bit with plain rings, and mouthpiece in three parts, namely, two lateral branches each with very stout rounded external

[1] *Archaeologia*, xvi. 348, pl. L.
[2] *Ass. Arch. Soc. Reports*, xviii. 59, pl. VII. 8.
[3] *Journal Brit. Arch. Ass.* xv. 227, pl. 22.
[4] *Hull Museum Publication*, no. 47; *Yorks. Arch. Journal*, xix. 487.
[5] *Archaeologia*, lx. 281, fig. 22.

knobs, through which the ring passes, while at the inner ends are loops connected by an 8-shaped link, round the middle of which is a ribbed collar. On each ring, on either side of the knob of the lateral branch, is a stud, evidently intended in the first instance to prevent the ring from running round in the end of the branch, though, as in most specimens the portion of the ring on which the mouthpiece works is thinner than the remainder of the ring, the reason for the studs is not quite clear. However, as some of these Celtic bits are made of iron plated with bronze, the knobs may have served to keep the ends of the mouthpiece from chafing the edges of the bronze tubing which encased the iron ring.

(*b*) The Polden hoard supplies another stage in which the mouthpiece is in two links only, one half having its inner loop set at right angles to that of the corresponding link, so doing away with the necessity of the third element.[1] This amounts to a normal snaffle-bit, and continues in use right through the period, and has no actual bearing on the otherwise peculiar development followed by the first class.

(*c*) The main feature of this development is the amalgamation of the lateral branches with the rings, reducing the whole bit to three elements, namely, the rings as before with excrescent bars and a connecting link, this latter lengthened to compensate for the loss involved by the absorption of the branches into the ring. This absorption takes the form, as it were, of drawing back the branch into the interior of the ring, so that the ring now meets the branch at what would

---

[1] *B.M. Guide* (*Iron Age*), 143, fig. 162. The hoard contains fourteen such bits, of which twelve form six pairs for double harness.

originally have been its middle. The result is well seen in examples from the Stanwick hoard. Naturally there would have been no point in retaining the great thickness of the end of the branch in its first state; this is therefore flattened down to a thickness closely approximating to that of the ring itself, though in the rounded ornamental portions within the ring of a bit from Seven Sisters we seem to have a reminiscence of the bulbous end of the branch. Equally naturally this projection of the branch into the interior of the ring soon lends itself to a variety of decorative elaboration, often in consonance with that employed on other parts of the harness.

In the bit from Rise, Yorkshire,[1] the same flattening has taken place, but the portion inside the ring, even though the bit, as has been said already, is certainly considerably later than the Stanwick bits, has on one side retained the knob-like end of the branch in its original position. But this bit, as all the Stanwick examples and others besides, illustrates the practice of decorating one ring more elaborately than the other, the reason being that bits with dissimilarly ornamented rings formed part of a double set of harness in which the more elaborate ends were visible on the outside of the pair of horses. The rings in the Seven Sisters hoard show how in the more elaborate ring the basis of this decoration had been almost or entirely forgotten, since the ornamental filling of the ring is only connected to the ring opposite the loop to which the mouthpiece was attached by a tenuous bar, which has no resemblance to the shank of the original branch. This is not always the case, as demonstrated by the admirable bit from

[1] *B.M. Guide* (*Iron Age*), 103, pl. VIII.

Birrenswark, Dumfriesshire.[1] That it is somewhat later
than the Seven Sisters examples is proved by the
presence of little leaflets in the decoration, arranged in
a classical manner. Furthermore, the enamel was in
two colours, and not merely red as usually stated. The
second colour was, I think, yellow, in accordance with
a fashion very prevalent on objects of the second century
in Scotland. Even here we may note the presence of the
Celtic touch in the little Z-like motive with eyes in each
limb, a development from the similar S-shaped motive
frequent on earlier Celtic work.

(d) Even in the bit with two links the process of
absorption can be illustrated by a bit from the Thames,[2]
which was originally decorated with enamel in lozenges
and triangles, presumably in two colours. Here a cruciform plate is incorporated in the circumference of the
ring itself, and in order to overcome a difficulty in
joining the mouthpiece to the rings the outer ends of
the links have no loops, but are curved and hooked
through the loop on the ring and secured by a large stud
or boss decorated with a well-known Celtic triangular
pattern.

(e) In the north occurs a variation of the Rise type
which seems to have aimed at reproducing the same
effect as that of the Rise bit without the employment of
enamel. The best example belongs to a hoard of harness
from Middlebie, Dumfriesshire.[3] The shape of the
filling of the rings closely resembles that of the Rise
bit, with rounded leaves drawn to a point at their outer

[1] J. Anderson, *Scotland in Pagan Times (Iron Age)*, 123, fig. 101;
Proc. Soc. Ant. Scot. xv. 320, fig. 4.

[2] *Proc. Soc. Ant.* xxiii, fig. opp. 159.

[3] *Soc. Ant. London, Coll. Drawings*, ii. 61; D. Wilson, *Archaeology
and Prehistoric Annals of Scotland*, 458.

end and with the same well-marked ridge dividing the point. The middle is filled with a large, perfectly plain boss. This style of ornamentation is particularly common in sites along the Wall and in lowland Scotland, as at Newstead and at Traprain Law, and occurs not only on harness, but also on a whole series of fastenings, and from the evidence of Newstead must belong to the second century, surviving to the time of its evacuation in A.D. 180. The same well-marked feature is also present on the bit from Place Fell, Westmorland,[1] and makes it impossible to date it to the century between 50 B.C. and A.D. 50, as Mr. Hawkes has done.[2] It cannot be earlier than the latter half of the first century A.D. and is more likely for the reasons given above to belong to the second.

Subsequently bronze bits apparently went out of fashion, for with the exception of one rather special example from Ireland,[3] those described seem to have no successors. This brings us to the bridle-bits as they normally appear in Ireland, since they furnish an additional piece of evidence for the time at which the Celtic culture of the period under review must have made its way to Ireland. Already we have found that there is reason to believe that it had passed across the Irish Channel by way of the east coast of England and the lowlands of Scotland. It is interesting to observe in confirmation of this that the same find at Ulceby, Lincolnshire, which contained part of a bit of the Hagbourne Hill type also contained the ring of another.

[1] *Ant. Journ.* ix. 41–2.
[2] Kendrick and Hawkes, *Archaeology in England and Wales, 1914–1931*, p. 191.
[3] *Journal Kilkenny and South East of Ireland Arch. Soc.*, n.s. i. 422, coloured plate.

This ring, now in Liverpool Museum, is of iron sheathed in bronze, and in addition to two studs decorated with small bosses in a ring round a central boss of a slightly larger size, it still retains the bulbous end of the branch of the mouthpiece.[1] This is ornamented in relief with an intricate design of thin scrolls broken at intervals by small bosses. In the British Museum is a complete bit from Ireland which in place of the two small studs has two large spherical studs treated in a manner almost identical with that employed on the branch of the Ulceby bit. Further than this, the Irish bit is built up on the model of the Hagbourne Hill type, that is, with two branches connected at the middle by a short link. It is noteworthy that, in spite of modifications of detail peculiar to Ireland, the whole range of bridle-bits in the Irish collections, with the exception of the special piece referred to above, preserve throughout the general form of the Hagbourne Hill bit, with its three links and two studs, usually of small size, on the ring. These last, again, whether or no their purpose was still understood, retain their original position on the ring and have not, as on the Rise bit and other pieces, been moved to a point where they lose their functional purpose and become mere adjuncts to the ornamentation.

The terrets. Many of the earlier types of terrets have already been cited and figured by way of illustration of the art and craftsmanship of an earlier period. Those with the wide band, decorated with enamel, are *sui generis* and have little subsequent history. But there are other early examples, also enamelled, which belong to a series which has as long a history as the bridle-bits.

(*a*) They begin probably with a perfectly plain sub-

[1] *Journal Brit. Arch. Ass.* xv. 225, pl. 22. 1.

oval ring of stout bronze, round in section; such occur
on early, as at Glastonbury and Polden Hill, as well as
on later sites. Terrets of the same simple form, but
decorated, are equally early in this country. Examples
may be cited again from Hagbourne Hill, Hunsbury,
the King's Barrow at Arras, from Glastonbury, and
elsewhere. The decoration takes the form in the first
instance of a series of rounded indentations or knobs
of a simple kind. At Hagbourne Hill there is a row of
well-defined bosses alternating with curved depressions.
At Glastonbury the bosses have, as it were, been split
in two, producing the effect of a pair of lips, and it is
this modification which gives rise to the future development of the terret for the next 300 years.

(*b*) At the next stage the ring loses its depressions on
the upper face and is made of a plain bar, round or oval
in section, usually increasing in girth towards the collars
which define the junction of the ornamental part of the
ring with the bar by which it was affixed to the harness.
The prominent feature now is the lips, which show a
great increase in size, projecting far above the edge of
the ring and fashioned with vertical outer edges. The
terrets are sometimes left plain like the example from
Polden Hill already mentioned and others in the Stanwick hoard, but are frequently decorated both on the lips
and also on the side with champlevé enamel, invariably
red. The decoration generally consists of spots, small or
large, sometimes of triangular motives, often made to
follow the curves of the body of the terret; the enamel
is frequently heightened by engraved lines or panels of
punched dots. Where the girth of the ring and the size
of the lips decrease, we are face to face with the decadence of the type. This is to be seen on one example

from Polden Hill,[1] on the pair from Stanton, Suffolk,[2] on those belonging to three of the four sets of trappings in the Stanwick hoard,[3] and on one from Newstead, Peeblesshire.[4]

(c) In the second class, as in the decorated examples of the first, the lips, as we have seen, were set transversely to the ring. At Polden Hill and in an isolated specimen from Leicester we meet with an important modification. The lips are now set in the same plane as the ring itself; and this allowed the number of lips to be increased to three or even four, set fan-wise on the fore-edge of the ring; the lips in this case are of uniform thickness throughout and moderately thin; they usually have a groove round their edge. Generally all the lips are of the same size; in some cases, however, the two inner are rather smaller than the two outer. On one terret they are very much smaller, and the outer lips have been depressed until they practically constitute a disk placed on the top of the ring with a pair of lips springing from the middle of it. The decoration of many of these is more elaborate. Spots with panels of punched dots are still used on the ring, but on the face of the two inner lips we find an arrangement of enamel which, if the lips were flattened down, would present itself as a roundel with an enamelled quatrefoil. One

---

[1] *Archaeologia*, xiv. 92, pl. xx. 5.

[2] British Museum.

[3] That illustrated in the *B.M. Guide* (*Iron Age*), fig. 151, is the exception. By the courtesy of the officials of the Department of British and Mediaeval Antiquities in the British Museum, I was permitted to make a minute examination of the Stanwick hoard, and was able to distinguish clearly the principal constituents of the four sets; they have now been arranged according to the division of the hoard made by me after that examination.

[4] James Curle, *Newstead*, pl. LXXV. 2.

example from Polden Hill actually has the midmost of three groups of lips thus accidentally flattened, and the quatrefoil-like design can be clearly seen (pl. I. 2).

(*d*) It is exactly along these lines that the terret subsequently develops. An example from Seven Sisters, Neath, has three knobs set with rounded bosses of enamel, in two colours, a yellow quatrefoil in a red ground (pl. II. 2). Commonly, however, the top of the knob is flat, and in such specimens, as on one from Saham Toney, Norfolk, the ring is rectangular in section and sometimes has its upper side decorated with enamel. A variation occurs in terrets belonging to the set which on all stylistic grounds must be the latest among the trappings in the Stanwick hoard. These are still decorated in the old manner with spots of red enamel, but they are quite small and are placed along the sides of the ring, as also is the case with another specimen belonging to another set of trappings in the same hoard, with the old style of transverse lips, probably here a survival. In the former set the terrets (and again an example from Traprain Law) have, however, six flat-topped knobs, but here, it is to be noted, arranged in three pairs.

A note may here be added in regard to terrets as a whole. From the evidence afforded by the Stanwick hoard it seems certain that in a set of double harness there were five terrets, namely two pairs with the wider face of the bar at the base of the ring set vertically, and one larger ring with a bar, often in the shape of a lozenge, slightly concave underneath and set with its wide face in a horizontal position. Though less easy to distinguish, some of the terrets in the Polden Hill hoard seem to admit of the same grouping of four small examples and one large, and it is well illustrated in the earlier Westhall group.

(*e*) A variety of class (*d*) has knobs of rectangular or oval form, usually enamelled and three in number. No two examples are exactly similar, and the class seems to represent a decadent mixture of the features of classes (*c*) and (*d*) with the jewelled appearance in some cases advanced a stage beyond that of the Seven Sisters specimen by the addition of blue. The Colchester terret mentioned above (p. 104), though without knobs, falls stylistically into this class.

(*f*) In northern Britain, and particularly in proximity to Hadrian's Wall, a terret in which the ring is decorated with plain round knobs occurs with some frequency, and may be regarded as characteristic of that region, where it is in full consonance with the 'boss' style referred to above in the account of the bit from Middlebie. Usually with only three knobs, they also occur with four, the middle two set, as at Middlebie, fairly close to one another, or absolutely touching, as on an example from Traprain Law. One in the National Museum of Scottish Antiquities (DWA 2) from Easter Wooden Farm, Eckford, Roxburghshire, has three knobs, but each of these is itself formed of three knobs arranged round the sides and top of the ring in contact with one another.

(*g*) The terrets so far examined for the most part have a bar of the same metal (bronze) as the rest of the ring. Nevertheless both the simple earlier types, whether quite plain or with incipient lips, as also the broad highly enamelled class, sometimes have their bars made of iron. It would seem therefore that the iron bar is not an absolutely reliable criterion of date. On the other hand, it is normal in a class of terrets in which the ring is slender at the top, but increases rapidly in girth to its base, which has had, as it were, a piece of the metal sliced off, leaving a large oval opening in which the iron bar is concealed. Above the base is a projection of varying size; it may be only a slight point, or somewhat larger and broader and vertically ribbed, or it may be quite tall and bifurcated at the top, in all cases leaving a more or less kidney-shaped opening in the ring. The suggestion that this class is late seems to be borne out by the fact that in some specimens, as in one from Towie, Aberdeenshire, the iron bar has been run in with lead.

If this type with the concealed bar is, as it may well be, of second or even third century date, it gives a clue to the date of the two enamelled specimens from the Fayoum and from Eauze, South France now in the British Museum. It has been claimed by M. Étienne Michon[1] that they are really foreign and, instead of being exports from Britain, as suggested in the account of the Fayoum example,[2] they are rather the prototype of the whole British broad type. But the decoration of simple hooked scrolls is a commonplace of Roman design, and the combination of enamel in red and light blue is introduced in the Roman period and is not employed earlier. Even the design on the side of the base of the Fayoum example, a square divided by wavy diagonals, can be paralleled in green and yellow(?) enamel on the oblate-faced knobs of an example of class (e) (now in the Black Gate Museum

[1] Ant. Journ. v. 145.
[2] Proc. Soc. Ant. xx. 57; B.M. Guide (Iron Age), 87, fig. 81.

at Newcastle). Finally, an imperfect terret of the same form from London is preserved in the Guildhall Museum.

Such are the chief varieties of terrets found in Great Britain during the space of some 300 or 400 years. It is interesting to note their distribution, as it coincides very closely with the trend of historical events before and after the conquest (fig. 33).

1. The simpler examples are found on many sites, but occur at such places as Hod Hill, Glastonbury, Hunsbury, and Hunmanby, East Riding, Yorkshire. The beaded variety is known from Hod Hill and Hunsbury, while the initial stage of the type with incipient lips comes from Hagbourne Hill. Those with full lips come from Hod Hill, Arras, and one from the Saxon cemetery at Fairford.[1] Some of the plainer rings have a line of ornamentation round their outer edge, as at Glastonbury and Cadbury Castle, Somerset, and Richborough, Kent.[2] All seem to belong to the region in which the earlier remains of Celtic occupation have come to light.

2. The broad, enamelled type is practically confined to south-eastern England. They occur at Bapchild and Richborough, Kent; at Westhall and an unknown site in Suffolk (Ashmolean Museum); the Thames at Runnymede, and at Colchester,[3] Essex. An isolated specimen outside this area, now in Edinburgh, came from Auchendolly, Dumfriesshire.

3. The lipped terrets have a wider distribution.

---

[1] W. M. Wylie, *Fairford Graves*, pl. v. 7.

[2] H. St. George Gray and A. Bulleid, *Glastonbury*, 230, fig. 45 *c*; J. P. Bushe-Fox, *Richborough*, i, pl. XIII. 16.

[3] Colchester Museum, 596P.03 from Castle Park and 1406.07 from the Union Grounds.

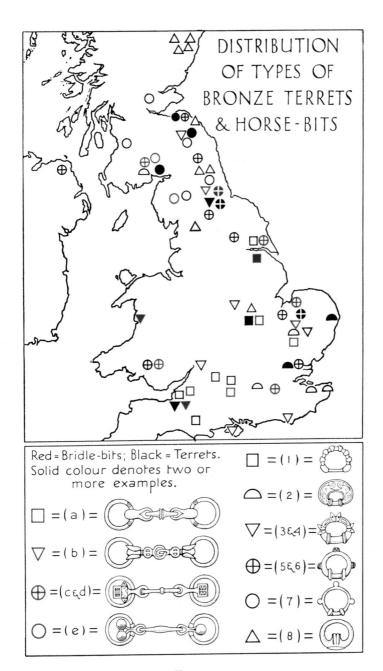

Red = Bridle-bits; Black = Terrets.
Solid colour denotes two or
more examples.

□ = (a) =

▽ = (b) =

⊕ = (c&d) =

○ = (e) =

□ = (1) =

⌒ = (2) =

▽ = (3&4) =

⊕ = (5&6) =

○ = (7) =

△ = (8) =

DISTRIBUTION
OF TYPES OF
BRONZE TERRETS
& HORSE-BITS

FIG. 33.

They are known from Kingsholm (Gloucestershire),[1] Polden Hill (Somerset), Alfriston (Sussex), Stanton (Suffolk), Stanwick (Yorkshire), and from Newstead (Peeblesshire).

4. The type with lips in the same plane as the rings occurs at Polden Hill, in a Jutish grave on Chessel Down, Isle of Wight,[2] and at Leicester.[3]

5. Terrets with round or flat-topped knobs decorated with a quatrefoil in enamel are known from Seven Sisters, Neath; Saham Toney,[4] Norfolk; the Cambridgeshire Fens; Colchester, Essex; Stanwick, Yorkshire, and, without enamel, from County Antrim, North Ireland (Greenwell Collection, British Museum).

6. The variety assigned to this class occurs at Saham Toney,[5] Fremington Hagg, near Reeth, Swaledale, Yorkshire (a fragment;[6] from the same site come several pieces of the niello-work found at Hod Hill and Seven Sisters); from the site of the North-Eastern Railway Station at York, 1878 (York Museum); from Great Chesters (Newcastle) and from High Rochester (Bremenium; now in Alnwick Castle Museum).[7]

7. The class with round knobs has been found at Kirkby Thore, Yorkshire,[8] Muircleuch, near Lauder, Berwickshire,[9] Eckford, Roxburghshire,[10] Middlebie,

---

[1] *Glastonbury*, 231 (Bristol Museum).
[2] *V.C.H.*, *Hants*, i. 389, fig. 19.
[3] *Arch. Cambrensis*, 1905, fig. opp. p. 130; *V.C.H.*, *Leics.*, i. 173.
[4] *V.C.H.*, *Norfolk*, i, pl. opp. p. 273, top left and bottom left.
[5] Ibid., top right.
[6] York Museum; Clarkson, *History of Richmond* (1821), 13–16.
[7] *Catalogue of the Antiquities at Alnwick Castle*, 145, no. 776.
[8] *Archaeologia*, xxxi. 285. To judge from the figure it has been adapted to form a buckle or brooch.
[9] *Proc. Soc. Ant. Scot.* lv. 17, fig. 4.
[10] Ibid. lxvi. 365.

Dumfriesshire,[1] Traprain Law, Haddingtonshire,[2] and possibly Ardoch, Perthshire.[3]

8. Finally, the plain type with enclosed iron bar is known from Giggleswick, Yorkshire, Corbridge and Chesters, Northumberland,[4] Eyemouth, Berwickshire,[5] Towie[6] and Inverurie,[7] Aberdeenshire. Others without provenance are in the British Museum. There, too, is preserved the only southern occurrence of the type known to me, namely from Billing, Northamptonshire.

To the first centuries of the Roman occupation of Britain must be assigned the special group of penannular and spiral bronze armlets peculiar to Scotland.[8] Only one, and that from North Ireland, near Newry, County Down,[9] has been found outside that country, and even there they come for the most part from the region stretching from the Forth to Aberdeen. The decoration of the surface of these ungainly objects is effected by dividing the surface into a series of panels delimited by narrow, curving beads in relief, sometimes of elongated, lentoid form, sometimes terminating in

---

[1] *Soc. Ant. London, Coll. Drawings*, ii. 61; Daniel Wilson, *Archaeology and Prehistoric Annals of Scotland*, 458.

[2] *Proc. Soc. Ant. Scot.* xlix. 181, fig. 131; lvi. 222, fig. 20. 8.

[3] Ibid. xxxii. 461, fig. 11; imperfect, but at any rate, if plain, a large slim type that also occurs at Middlebie.

[4] *Yorks. Arch. Journal*, xxii. 237; *Corbridge*, 1910, p. 46, pl. IV, fig. 1; *Catalogue of Roman Antiquities at Chesters* (1907), no. 832.

[5] *Royal Commission of the Ancient and Historical Monuments of Scotland (County of Berwick)*, xxxviii. The Rev. R. H. Lamont, Minister of Coldingham, in answer to inquiries about its form very kindly sent the piece for my inspection.

[6] *Proc. Soc. Ant. Scot.* v. 341 and fig.; xv. 321, fig. 5; *Cat. Nat. Mus. Scottish Ant.* FA 30–1.

[7] *B.M. Guide (Iron Age)*, 158, fig. 189.

[8] They are almost all illustrated in Joseph Anderson, *Scotland in Pagan Times (Iron Age)*, figs. 115–40.

[9] *Proc. Soc. Ant. Scot.* xv. 362, fig. 31.

trumpet-like ends, and by further dividing the panels
thus formed by the insertion of short, lentoid bars, also
in relief, in some cases curiously anticipating the insertion of little spots of the same shape in the enamelled
escutcheons of a later period of Celtic art in England,
though it would be difficult to trace any actual connexion between their use in the two styles.

The more massive examples of the armlets are
penannular, and terminate in large circular terminals, in
the centre of which was an orifice for the insertion of a
circular enamelled plaque. These are unfortunately in
most examples now missing, but two armlets, namely
that from Drummond Castle, Perthshire, in the British
Museum,[1] and that from Castle Newe, Aberdeenshire,[2]
have their plaques preserved. In the former the design
differs on the two armlets; one may best be described
as a four-pointed star in red with a yellow pellet at its
centre, superimposed on a yellow quatrefoil, all on a red
ground; the other has a yellow Latin cross with a red
pellet at its middle, also on a red ground. Those from
Castle Newe (fig. 34) have only one design, a chequy
pattern in red and yellow. The rosetti-form motive takes
us back at once to the rosette which we have seen became
a feature of the decoration of terrets at about the middle
of the first century and certainly persisted to the close
of the century, if not longer. The armlets seem to prove
that it did; they also conserved the combination of red
and yellow enamel, which came into vogue at the
same time.

It is not easy to cite other examples in this same style,

---

[1] *B.M. Guide (Iron Age)*, 155, fig. 186.
[2] *Proc. Soc. Ant. Scot.* xv. 330, fig. 10, now in the possession of Oscar
Raphael Esq., F.S.A.

but there is one little group, three in number, of oblong plaques with rounded ends—to judge from one example used possibly as belt-plates—that have some claim to

FIG. 34. Bronze armlet with enamelled disks from Castle Newe, Aberdeenshire.

be regarded as productions of the same school. One is illustrated from a cast in the collections of the Society of Antiquaries, by Romilly Allen in his *Celtic Art*.[1] Though he does not specifically place the object itself in the eleventh century, he does include it in his survey of Celtic art of the Christian period. At the same time

[1] Plate opposite p. 170, where he compares its decoration with that of the cover of the Stowe Missal made between A.D. 1023 and 1052. Where the original is preserved is unknown to the writer.

he remarks on the pronouncedly Celtic character of the trumpet-shaped expansions of the curved designs on the rounded ends. Fortunately, other specimens give us a better idea of their real date. The specimen illustrated by Romilly Allen has at the middle what he describes as a square panel of triangular pierced work. This, again, is incorrect. The panel-decoration consists of a diagonal pattern of triangles, evidently decorated in two colours of champlevé enamel.[1]

The second example comes from Drumashie, near Dores, Inverness-shire.[2] In form it closely resembles the last, but the trumpet-like expansions are reduced to a pair of repoussé half-bosses, unconnected with the orifice at each end of the plate, which in the other specimen is surrounded by the curve of the scroll to which the trumpet-ends are attached. The Drumashie piece has its enamelled plaque preserved, ornamented with a cruciform design, in the nature of a St. Andrew's cross with lentoid arms, in red within a background of yellow. The design strongly recalls the rosetti-form motive on the Drummond Castle armlet.

The third example is an imperfect specimen in the Museum at York, consisting of part of the framework with its ends decorated in a manner similar to, but slightly stiffer than that of the first of these plates. The provenance is not given; the enamelled plate from the middle is wanting. Yet it may be surmised that it was found in York, for among the objects discovered in excavations on the North-Eastern Railway in 1873 is a square plaque decorated with horizontal lines of

[1] The photograph indicates that in alternate rows the enamel is missing, as frequently happens when two colours are used, one evidently being more perishable than the other.

[2] *Proc. Soc. Ant. Scot.* lviii. 12, fig. 1.

triangles in alternate red and yellow enamel, which in my opinion belongs to the imperfect framework.

The colouring and style of the enamels has much in common with those of the Scottish armlets; and the treatment of the repoussé work also closely compares in both cases. They must surely belong to the same school. For their date we have the additional evidence of the discovery at Drumashie of one of those fastenings to which I have alluded above as so often decorated in the 'boss' style. That from Drumashie[1] has, on the contrary, a squared end ornamented with nine small squares of red and yellow enamel, as on the belt-plate.[2] Not only were plain and enamelled examples of this form found at Traprain Law, but also the moulds in which some of them were cast. They were found at levels which were dated as late as the end of the third century, but in the main the evidence points to a somewhat earlier date. If the former were correct, the gulf between this style and the escutcheons of a later period is appreciably narrowed.

From Ballymoney, County Antrim (Ashmolean Museum, Evans Coll.) comes a massive bronze link, in the form of a figure of eight with its waist prolonged into a stem with ribbed mouldings. It may conceivably be associated with the above style. On the loops are lip-like mouldings which, though not exactly similar,

---

[1] Loc. cit., fig. 2.

[2] The enamel is in exactly the same style as that of the oblong boss on the fragment of a terret from Traprain Law (ibid. lvi. 258, fig. 24. 3). The example from Bowland, Gala Water, Midlothian (*Proc. Soc. Ant. Scot.* lvii. 14, fig. 3) of that specially British form of bijouterie, the fibula in the shape of a roosting cock, is enamelled in the same gay colours. Specimens from more southerly sites are decorated in red and blue or other more sober combinations of colour. The Celtic preference for red and yellow still prevailed in the north.

are strongly reminiscent of the treatment of some of the
lentoid mouldings on the Scottish armlets. A slight
difference in character may be due to the variant
method of production, casting as contrasted with repoussé work. The same may be said of a scabbard-
chape from Houndslow, Westruther, Berwickshire,[1]
which has trumpet mouldings round an oval opening
not unlike those of the York belt-plate.

There is one other object from Scotland that I suspect has to be associated with the bronze armlets and
other pieces decorated in this style. It is the gold ornament from Shaw Hill, near Cairnsmuir, Kirkurd,
Peeblesshire.[2] The work is far more delicate than that
of the bronze, but it has nevertheless several traits in
common, as Anderson justly observed. In addition to
small bosses and spiral coils, it has its surface broken
up into panels by curving lines in repoussé, sometimes
with trumpet-ends. On the back, which is otherwise
unornamented, there is a small panel filled with bosses
and enclosed with a trumpet-ended semicircle similar
to that on the York belt-plate, while the lower edge of
the object is bounded by a transversely ribbed wire,
comparable with that encircling the middle of the Drummond Castle armlet.

One object from Wales, the imperfect gold-plated
fibula from Tre'r Ceiri, Carmarthenshire,[3] is in the same
style. It serves to corroborate the centrifugal nature of
this development in relation to the conquest, and at the
same time provides in its form as a derivative from the
thistle-brooch a date towards the close of the first century.

[1] *Proc. Soc. Ant. Scot.* lv. 19, fig. 5.
[2] J. Anderson, op. cit. 138, fig. 114.
[3] R. M. Wheeler, op. cit. 213, fig. 90.

But where did this style originate? There is little resembling it among works of the same or an earlier period in England. The nearest that might be cited—and even it only offers a faint resemblance—is the disk from Kingsholm, Gloucestershire (p. 54). The decoration of the armlets, when seen on a developed sketch (fig. 35 a),[1] suggests perhaps that it is not unconnected with the evolution of the broken-backed curve, and in point of date there is nothing inherently impossible in such an explanation. But the generality of South British work in that style hardly provides the necessary links in the chain of development; for them I am inclined to look elsewhere.

One splendid product of Celtic art in the British Isles has so far been left unmentioned, namely the magnificent gold collar from Broighter, County Derry, Ireland, described in 1897 by Sir Arthur Evans.[2] Here we see the same class of decoration, but in point of execution it far transcends any of the work on the Scottish examples. It is an entirely admirable piece of skilled goldsmith's work. Against the background of minutely engraved compass-lines (fig. 35 b) the curves of the repoussé design swing in harmonious beauty, swelling here and there to trumpet-mouldings, defined from one another by graceful, lentoid bosses, while in places the scheme is broken by reflex curves, leading to a medley of coils and swellings along the median line, among which one seems to recognize a remembrance of the 𝒮-shaped motive, which is so prominent a feature of the engraved mirrors and other objects of an earlier period. The little spiral coils set in the centres of these median motives are just those which appear on the gold

[1] e.g. J. Anderson, op. cit., figs. 120 and 123.
[2] *Archaeologia*, lv. 391 ff. and pl. XXII.

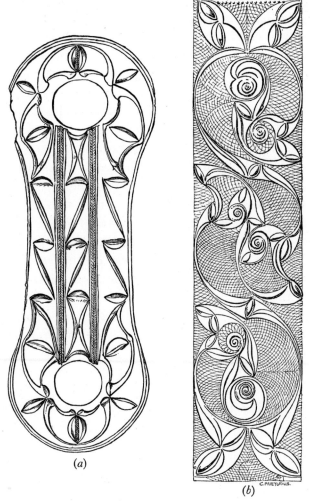

(a)

(b)

C. PRÆTORIUS.

FIG. 35. (a) Development of ornamentation of bronze armlet from Drumside, Belhelvie, Aberdeenshire; (b) development of ornamentation of gold torc from Broighter, County Derry.

ornament from Shaw Hill, and it is that object which serves to link this collar with the whole Scottish group which we have been examining.

But one difficulty arises. The form of the collar and its peculiar mode of T-fastening can, as Sir Arthur Evans observed, be paralleled from numerous continental examples. For the form we may cite that from Frasnes-lez-Buissenal, Hainaut, Belgium,[1] and the mode of fastening is, as Sir Arthur Evans noted, the same as that employed on torcs from Aquitaine. These Gaulish torcs are assigned by Déchelette to la Tène II, and thus to a period considerably anterior to that with which we are dealing. The Belgian collar was, however, found in association with Gallic coins, and those of a class assigned by Blanchet to the first century B.C.; they appear in Britain at that date. The form of the collar is not, therefore, necessarily la Tène II; the associated coins point to la Tène III. But apart from that, I see no valid reason for placing some of the Aquitanian series so early, and especially that from Fenouillet, Haute-Garonne.[2] The whole style of the torc, with its row of disks strung on the hoop at its points of fastening, recalls at once the group of British torcs strung with bronze disks and beads in a similar manner, and they, as we have seen, belong to the time of the conquest and later.[3]

The decoration of the Irish collar, moreover, is a brilliant exposition of the style of the broken-backed curve in its initial stages, that phase of treatment of the

[1] Déchelette, *Manuel*, ii. 1337, fig. 586.
[2] Illustrated in *Archaeologia*, lv, fig. 6, as coming from Serviés-en-Val, near Carcassonne.
[3] In any case the fastening once devised would have no reason to die out immediately, as its use for dating purposes would suggest.

curve by Celtic artists in Britain, that contained within it all the preconditions for the evolution of the true trumpet-scroll. It was, as Sir Arthur Evans also observed, the result of the compass-work which was an essential of Celtic ornament. He refers to the bone flakes, some of them possibly trial-pieces from the so-called Tomb of Ollamh Fodhla, or Sliabh na Caillighe, County Meath.[1] They are decorated with designs in which the elements of that employed on the collar can be clearly detected, especially the two left-hand examples in the bottom row on p. 56 of Conwell's work. In other respects they seem to mark an earlier phase in the development of the style, and it is in this that their chief interest lies.

The same may be said of some of the fibulae found in Ireland.[2] They represent a rather specialized development of la Tène I and la Tène II forms, and are clearly to be regarded as derivatives with a long history behind them. Even the earliest typologically are widely separated from their continental prototypes. Equally clearly at the end of this localized series must fall examples furnished with hinged pins in place of spring-coils. It is just these that are decorated with mouldings in the style of the torc and of the trial-pieces cited above.

Throughout the history of pre-Christian Celtic art, as indeed to some extent in Christian times, it is possible to detect evidences of close connexions between Ireland, particularly the north-east, and Scotland, as well as the tract of northern England adjacent to the Border. It has already been suggested that the art of the objects found at Lisnacroghera is an offshoot of a style which was

[1] E. A. Conwell, *Discovery of the Tomb of Ollamh Fodhla*, 53 ff.
[2] *Journal R. Soc. Ant. Ireland*, liii. 13, fig. 8, especially nos. 6, 7, and 8.

transported thither by way of the Tyne gap and Galloway, the nearest point to the coast of Ireland.

I am, therefore, inclined to the opinion that the whole group under immediate examination is the outcome of a specialized development of Celtic ornament, common to northern Britain and north-east Ireland in the first century of our era. The Irish collar is perhaps the earliest work of this school that we possess, though the gold ornament from Shaw Hill approaches closely to it. Minor products, executed by engraving on flat surfaces like the Sliabh na Caillighe bone flakes, can be seen on the handles of the Irish spoons[1] and that from Burnmouth, Berwickshire,[2] as also a comb from Ghegan Rock, Seacliff,[3] and in another technique the open-work disk from Dowalton Loch crannog, Wigtownshire,[4] and lastly the Balmaclellan mirror, itself a moderately early product of the school.

Sir Arthur Evans[5] compares the snail-like coils on the Irish collar to the fine spiral sprays engraved on the Witham shield and other pieces in the same style. The gap between them, in point of time, is rather broad, but it may be that it is only the sparseness of our material that makes it difficult to span that gap with the eye of faith. I feel it may be claimed that this northern school of design comes into being in the first century B.C., but that in Scotland, except to some extent in Galloway, it tends to retreat northwards before the Roman advance, though still retaining its connexion with northern Ireland. In the eastern Lowlands and south of the Border it is largely replaced by the 'boss' style.

[1] *Arch. Journ.* xxvi. 64, figs. 11–15.
[2] *Proc. Soc. Ant. Scot.* lviii, 143, fig. 35; *Archaeologia* lxxvii. 106, fig. 11.   [3] *Cat. Nat. Mus. Scottish Ant.*, 1892, p. 246, HD 78.
[4] Ibid. 254, HU 62.   [5] Loc. cit. 388.

VI

THE REVIVAL

WE now come to what is the most obscure period in this extraordinary art-history. It would seem, from the evidence which I have passed under review for its existence during the first centuries of Roman rule in Britain, that the ornament was gradually declining from good to bad, from better to worse, and contained within itself all the germs of entire decay. Only in Ireland and in the unoccupied parts of Scotland, free as they were from Roman domination and the formalism of Roman art, though this applies less to Scotland than to Ireland, could there seem to be any hope of its survival and further development. It has, meanwhile, to be remembered that Roman rule connoted a large measure of non-interference with native life, in accordance with Roman practice in its dealings with its subjects, and that in consequence there was no inherent reason why Celtic art should not have also survived, even though only in an emasculated form, in Roman Britain also. We speak of an Art of the Dark Ages in Europe; we may here equally speak of a Dark Age of Celtic Art in Britain.

It is an incontestable fact—and one that still requires to be satisfactorily explained—that from about A.D. 250 to the end of the Roman period objects other than pottery which exhibit in any degree the influence of Celtic art in their decoration are distinguished by nothing so much as their scarcity.

One of the questions that will naturally rise to one's mind is where, if at any particular place in these islands, did the art first feel the fresh impetus which set it on the

road to the brilliant achievements of the eighth century
and onwards. In Scotland beyond the Forth, the style
which emerged in the gigantic armlets of the north-
east seems to have faded out entirely, leaving nothing
behind it.[1]

Nor is the case much better for Ireland; it is remarkable how little there is in that country that can be used
archaeologically to link up the sparse equivalents of the
earlier la Tène culture with the magnificent outburst of
the last three centuries of the first millennium. I have
shown above that certain types of bridle-bits are peculiar
to Ireland, and with them go those curious horse-
ornaments[2] one of which, in the National Museum in
Dublin, with a subovate head filled with a large stud
of red enamel, falls into line with a similar style in vogue
in northern England and southern Scotland from about
A.D. 50 onwards.

We are in fact confronted, to all appearance, by an
almost complete cessation of artistic production on the
part of the native, and, except that we have ample
evidence at a later stage of its powers of recuperation,
we should incline to believe that Celtic art was on the
high road to absolute extinction. But such was not
entirely the case. Here and there amid the darkness we
detect some spark, faint though it be, of the native
spirit which had informed the excellent work of pre-
Roman days, and, as we might reasonably expect, it is
in one of the minor arts, namely pottery, that the fires
of the ancient craftsmanship are still kept alive. Among
the classes of pottery assignable to the third and fourth

---

[1] J. Anderson, *Scotland in Pagan Times* (*Iron Age*), 141 ff.
[2] e.g. *Archaeologia,* lxvi. 349, pl. XXVII; *Journ. R. Soc. Ant. Ireland,*
liii, pl. III.

centuries two retain something of the old tradition. The so-called Castor ware, though also manufactured on the Continent, and though ornamented with figurative designs drawn from classical sources, yet in the presentation of those designs and especially in the accompanying scrolled ornament displays the impress of native aesthetic feeling. In a simpler degree the same holds good of the New Forest wares. Both are essentially provincial Roman in the matter of shapes; there the potter was working at the bidding of his masters, but in the decoration he was able to find some scope for his own predilections, lightening it by touches which can only have sprung from a freer and wilder spirit than that with which Roman art was imbued.

Apart from the pottery, almost the only objects about whose comparatively late date there seems to be some measure of agreement are certain small disk-brooches, on the face of which is soldered a thin plate of bronze embossed with a triskele-scroll design, such as those from Silchester, Berkshire,[1] Brough, Westmorland,[2] and Corbridge, Northumberland (fig. 36 a).[3] To these perhaps we may add certain enamelled disk-brooches decorated with a triskele design in two colours, for example, deep orange on blue from Silchester (Reading Museum), green on blue from Lowbury, Berkshire,[4] light blue on red, from Brough, Westmorland (Ashmolean Museum), and the same design developed into a five-limbed motive from Lowbury.[5] They seem to fit into this period rather than into the second century. The evidence cited by Professor Atkinson is not in itself convincing. The

---

[1] J. Romilly Allen, *Celtic Art*, fig. opp. p. 108.
[2] *Proc. Soc. Ant.* iv. 129.   [3] *Report for 1908*, fig. 22.
[4] D. Atkinson, *Lowbury*, pl. IX. 1.   [5] Op. cit. 35, pl. IX. 2.

second-century date was based on a Zugmantel dating, itself again somewhat wanting in definition. Mr. Collingwood,[1] while beginning the disk type in the second century, is prepared to carry its life beyond. The whole evidence in regard to third- and fourth-century finds is vague and still remains to be fully worked out. Pending definite proof to the contrary, the persistence of the type and of enamelling must be assumed. Certain combinations of colour used on the disk-brooches, as on other forms, bizarre in character, have the appearance of lateness; they produce the same impression as the groupings of colours employed on what is generally recognized as a late oval type.[2] Whatever may have been the case on the Continent—for, in spite of the undoubted survival of the glass industry, the impression left by some writers is that the craft of enamelling practically fell into disuse by the middle of the third century[3]—there can be no question about its survival in Britain, in view of the clear signs of its flourishing condition at a later date. It would in any event be unreasonable to suppose that all enamelling ceased in the second century in Britain, or even in the third. Philostratus's statement about enamelling can have no reference to the enamelled horse-trappings of the earlier Celtic work, as might be inferred from the context in which the passage is so often quoted. Philostratus was writing in the time of Septimius Severus (A.D. 197–211), so that the craft must still have been in full activity at

---

[1] *The Archaeology of Roman Britain*, 259.

[2] Blue and white, or black and red, e.g. Silchester (Reading Museum), with an intaglio of a human bust in a late barbarous style, executed, as Mlle Henry has pointed out to me, in the red enamel.

[3] O.R.L.I. Zugmantel, 80; *Der römische Limes in Österreich*, viii. 98 ff.

what is nearly the beginning of the dark period. The brightly coloured terrets and mounts were a thing of the past; the statement must rather be taken in reference to other works such as the large unfinished object in the British Museum,[1] or the bowl from Rudge, Wiltshire,[2] or that from Harwood, near Cambo, Northumberland.

The triskele ornament in the same style as on the little disk-brooches repeats itself on the strainer of a patella from Kyngadle, Llansadyrnin, Carmarthenshire,[3] associated, it is believed, with coins of Carausius, and again on a bronze mount from South Shields,[4] apparently the piece now in the Black Gate Museum at Newcastle, though not now complete as illustrated, and also on the lid of a seal-box in red on blue enamel from the site of the North-Eastern Railway at York (York Museum). There seem to exist ample indications that the Celtic designs were still in prevalent use.

Towards the close of the Roman period there comes into being in the north a style which Mr. Kendrick[5] has recently dubbed the 'Ultimate la Tène' style. This style calls for some notice here, since it serves as a milestone in the history of Celtic ornament. It appears commonly on penannular brooches, on hand-pins, on latchets, most of which are usually assigned to the sixth to eighth centuries; but, as will be seen, it certainly goes back earlier. The style as a whole is weak, arid in conception, executed mostly in tenuous ribbon-like scrolls and other motives, employed as a basis for

[1] *B.M. Guide to the Antiquities of Roman Britain*, pl. IX.
[2] *Catalogue of the Museum in Alnwick Castle*, p. 139, no. 476, col. plate, and p. 141.
[3] *Arch. Cambr.* vi. 1. 20 (1901). *Royal Commission of Ancient Monuments in Wales and Monmouthshire. Carmarthen*, 188, fig. 152.
[4] *Journal Brit. Arch. Ass.* xxix. 90, fig. 3.   [5] *Antiquity*, vi. 169.

champlevé enamel. It is a style in process of decadence, entirely devoid of the power to raise itself to a stronger growth without the assistance of some invigorating influence. But for all that, it still conserves the age-long Celtic predilection for curvilinear ornament.

It is a style which is by no means easy to translate into chronological terms. We have, however, two starting-points, one the class of circular brooches with applied disks embossed with scroll-pattern. These, as proved by their places of discovery, plainly belong to the Roman period, and they are assigned by Mr. Collingwood in his *Archaeology of Roman Britain* to the third century. That, I think, is too early. They are not only analogous in construction to several classes of continental brooches of the fourth century, but there appears on one of the examples from Brough a tendency which makes itself still more evident on non-Roman objects, namely, the transformation of the ends of the scrolls into a zoomorphic or ornithomorphic head.[1] This feature occurs repeatedly on some of the hand-pins of Ireland (fig. 36 b), usually assigned to the sixth to eighth centuries, as also on the well-known latchets[2] (fig. 36 c) in association with scrolls which in my opinion make it impossible to date the elaborate specimen from Dowris, County Offaly, in the British Museum[3] as late as Mr. Smith would place it. Above all it is very prominent on the remarkable horns from County Cork in Dublin (fig. 38 a).[4]

It is possible that some of these pieces, especially the

---

[1] Cf. J. Anderson, *Scotland in Early Times, Iron Age,* 161, fig. 141, on a stone ball from Walston, Lanark.

[2] e.g. W. 492 in Dublin Museum; G. Coffey, *Guide to the Celtic Antiquities of the Christian Period,* 2nd ed., fig. 15.

[3] *B.M. Guide to Anglo-Saxon Antiquities* (1923), fig. 172.

[4] *Journ. R. Soc. Ant. Ireland,* liii, 22, pl. II.

a

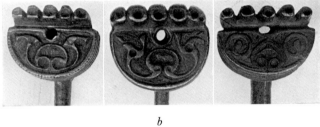

b

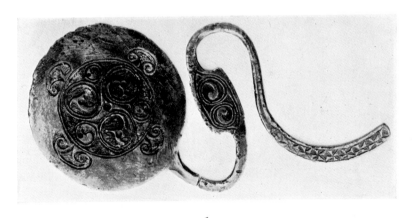

c

FIG. 36. (*a*) Embossed bronze brooches from Silchester, Berkshire, and Brough, Westmorland ($\frac{1}{1}$). British Museum. (*b*) Heads of bronze hand-pins from Ireland ($\frac{1}{1}$). National Museum of Ireland. (*c*) Bronze 'latchet' from Ireland ($\frac{1}{1}$). National Museum of Ireland.

hand-pins, may be earlier than the date usually assigned to them, but at best they represent a rather disjointed style, as can be clearly seen not only on the lunettes of the hand-pins, but also on the earlier examples of the penannular brooches.[1] The ornament becomes entirely subservient to the enamel, the fields of which are divided by its ribbon-like curves, occasionally enlarged into a rude head-finial. The appearance of this feature on these disk-brooches leaves us with insufficient material to bridge the gap of two centuries that would be required to take the Silchester brooch, for example, back to the second century.

The second starting-point is the hand-pin, the development of which has been traced by Mr. Reginald Smith.[2] Recent years have provided a valuable basis for its chronology in the finds at Traprain Law. There at least two stages in its evolution have come to light, covering on the evidence of coins a period from the late second down to the latter part of the fourth century. The variety with a circle of bosses forming a ring-head (fig. 32 g) goes back to the Antonines, but also occurs later,[3] while the type with a semicircle of bosses above and a crescentic plate below occurred at levels in which the coins ranged from Probus (A.D. 276–81) down to Constantine the Great and Magnentius,[4] and possibly even so late as the end of the fourth century (e.g. from the 1st level).[5] The last may possibly be no more than a chance occurrence at so high a level, as is suggested by

---

[1] e.g. G. Coffey, op. cit., figs. 22–5.

[2] *Opuscula Archaeologica Oscari Montelio septuagenario dicata,* *D. IX M. Sept. A. MCMXIII,* 280 ff. Stockholm, 1913.

[3] *Proc. Soc. Ant. Scot.* lvi, fig. 20, 1 (5 *a* level); lv, fig. 21, 7; and lvi, fig. 29, 4 (2nd level).

[4] Ibid. liv. 88–94, fig. 19 (2nd level).   [5] Ibid, 96, fig. 24.

the absence of specimens with any traces, even of the beginnings, of the zoomorphizing style, which, as we have
seen, actually appears on some of the repoussé-plated
brooches. The evidence goes to place this outbreak of a
zoomorphizing tendency at the very close of the Roman
period and its full development in the fifth century.
Unfortunately we have but few finds from which further
dating can be surmised—*proved* would be too strong a
term. It has been held[1] that the hand-pin in its most
elaborated form survives down to the eighth and even
tenth centuries, but evidence is not lacking to show that
a whole series of pins decorated in Mr. Kendrick's
'Ultimate la Tène' style must belong to the fifth
century.

The examination of this evidence brings us at once
into contact with the series of hanging-bowls decorated
with hooked escutcheons, which have been lately sub-
jected to a close and interesting analysis in the paper
cited above. Arguing from a study of the form of the
bowls themselves, Mr. Kendrick maintains that the
Wilton specimen[2] with its simple hollow rim, lacking
the flattened brim of other specimens, must stand early
in the series, and does not hesitate to place it as early as
the first half of the fifth century, and is even inclined to
throw it back to the fourth. The open-work decoration
of the escutcheon consisting of an arrangement of four
peltae set back to back in a quadripartite design is
clearly Roman in origin, and, as it is a motive common
enough in late Roman work on mosaics and the like,
his thesis is well grounded. Personally I incline a little
to the fifth century, since exactly the same combination

[1] R. A. Smith, op. cit. 289.
[2] G. Baldwin Brown, *Arts in Early England*, iv. 474, pl. cxviii.

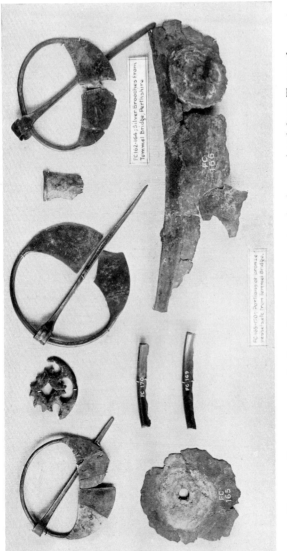

Fig. 37. Bronze penannular brooches and fragments of a bronze bowl from Tummel Bridge, Perthshire. National Museum of Scottish Antiquities, Edinburgh.

of bowl with primitive rim and escutcheons decorated
with an identical design occurs in a hoard found so far
north as Tummel Bridge, west of Pitlochry, Perthshire
(fig. 37).[1] In the original account it is described as a
brooch, but on a fragment of a bronze bowl found with it
the impress left by the disk before it became detached
from the bowl can be quite clearly detected. This
specimen, the most northerly occurrence of such bowls,
was associated with penannular brooches, a well-known
Celtic form, but, usually thought to be somewhat
later. Since, however, it is likely enough that the
bowl was loot gathered in a raid by the Picts to the
south, it can at least hardly be later than the fifth
century, and may well be even earlier, thus throwing
back the bowl and brooches still further towards
the Roman period. The same type of brooch occurs also in the hoard from Norries Law, Fifeshire,
which Mr. Smith has assigned to the sixth century.[2]
Here we find a hand-pin at just that stage of evolution
to which a century would bring its simpler predecessor
from Traprain Law. Moreover, the pin is decorated
in a style which falls into line with the zoomorphizing
phase to which allusion has been made above.[3]

It will hardly be then a matter for surprise to find that
escutcheons exist which are decorated in this selfsame
style, and, even though they come from so far south as
Faversham, Kent (fig. 39 *a, b*),[4] must be regarded as a
product of a northern workshop, since the style has

---

[1] *Proc. Soc. Ant. Scot.* xxii. 268.   [2] Loc. cit. 287.

[3] A plate in this hoard is embossed in a style identical with that
employed on Irish bronze disks (fig. 38 *b*), the design on which repeats
itself on the Cork horns. The hoard is surely earlier than it is generally
thought to be.

[4] *Antiquity*, vi, pl. v, fig. 5.

otherwise, to the best of my knowledge, no real existence in the south. There, as we shall see, an entirely
different style made itself prevalent.

It has to be remembered in dealing with this period
that political conditions were particularly favourable to
the growth or, if the term is permissible, re-growth of
more than one style. As we have noted, there was, even
under the Roman occupation, a strong Celtic feeling
prevailing in the north, and giving rise to an individual
school in Cumberland and the adjacent counties, while
in the civil province of the south, Roman life and
influences tended to relegate the Celtic element to
the background. It could hardly be expected that
these variant schools should have ceased their activities
immediately after the departure of the Romans. Indeed,
the evidence of the escutcheons argues entirely in the
contrary sense. As Mr. Kendrick has pointed out,
escutcheons from Dover and Mildenhall are essentially
classical in feeling, a feeling that never died out entirely
in the south. For, even after the Anglo-Saxon settlements were firmly established, there appear on the
jewellery of the invaders motives which have their
roots in a classical tradition, not imported by the invaders themselves, but revived, it would seem, from
native sources. In a short time, however, they fall
victims to Teutonic ornamental idiosyncrasies and lose
their individuality.

One has only to cast a glance over the names that
occur in the early history of the struggle between the
Anglo-Saxons and native Britons to realize that side by
side with a Romanized remnant (Ambrosius, &c.) among
the protagonists on the native side, and even strangely
enough it would appear also among the invaders, a

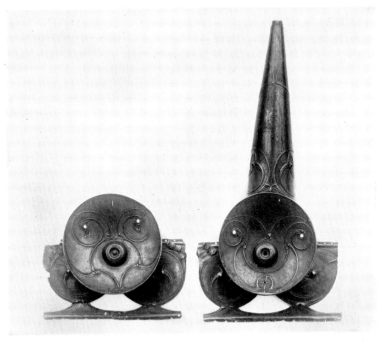

a

b

FIG. 38. (*a*) Bronze horned mounts from County Cork, Ireland, 6 in. high. (*b*) Bronze embossed disks from Ireland, 10–11 in. diam. National Museum of Ireland.

Celtic element (Vortigern, Ceadwalla, Cerdic, &c.) is very prominent. Gildas's account witnesses to a great Celtic revival after the departure of the Romans, one against which the Church had to struggle almost for its very existence. The same phenomenon is perceptible also in the sphere of artistic effort, and with it the contrast between north and south becomes very marked.

In the north the Ultimate la Tène style persisted, and is particularly well represented in southern Scotland and in Ireland. Here and there we meet with examples, rather less arid and tenuous in their expression than the generality of pieces ornamented in this style, and these are to be found rather on the nearer fringe of the artistic province. Amongst them I would place the escutcheons and base-ring from Barlaston, Staffordshire, for, though the swastika-like design on the former (fig. 39 c) rather inclines to the south, the design on the latter (as I think of linked peltae, not palmettes, and so a typical product of the period) repeats itself in disjointed form on many of the hand-pins and early penannular brooches.

The same motive in another combination appears on a fragment from Middleton Low,[1] Derbyshire, combined with elements which dominate the decoration of the escutcheons with which it was associated. To the northern group also belongs the Northumberland group, alike on grounds of locality and of style. They have one feature in particular in common both with the Barlaston escutcheons and with numerous products of the northern school, namely the use of millefiori inlay.

To the southern school belong by far the greater number of the escutcheons, remarkable alike in the variety and strength of the designs, the excellence of

---

[1] *Antiquity*, vi, pl. VIII. 2.

their technical production, and the amazing revival of the enameller's craft which they seem to represent, the last a sure sign that the craft must have been continuously practised even in a restricted measure throughout the Roman period and beyond. There can be no question that all the escutcheons were made in the British Isles; the only problem, the solution of which is still a matter of controversy, is in what particular part of the British Isles this work originated. The Faversham escutcheons already mentioned can at the moment only be regarded as a parallel, not as a line of descent. The want of satisfactory links, if any, with the earlier phases of Celtic art renders the problem yet more difficult, and such evidence as exists seems capable of several interpretations. Even then the point at issue will be found to be whether the art displayed on the escutcheons is a renaissance of Celtic art, or whether it has its roots elsewhere, and is in reality a creation independent of all Celtic tradition eventually absorbed by the Celts and by them blended with other ideas into what we know as Christian Celtic art.

Starting from the latter assumption, Mr. Kendrick distinguishes a group which with some justice he has called the 'Romanizing School', and in this group he places examples from Dover and Mildenhall, as well as others which I shall venture to group otherwise. The first two, are, it is true, decorated with motives purely classical in style, and elements of the same feeling also do appear in conjunction with scroll-patterns. Consequently it might fairly be argued, as it is by Mr. Kendrick, that these enamels with Romanizing designs are the basis from which the whole of the products of this southern school emerged. That may

a   *b*

c

FIG. 39. Enamelled bronze escutcheons ($\frac{1}{1}$). (*a*) and (*b*)
Faversham, Kent. (*c*) Barlaston, Staffordshire. British
Museum.

well be; but, as I hope to show, it is the spirit behind
the school that matters, not the initial products of a
particular phase.

Leaving on one side the 'Romanizing' series, we find
that the remaining examples of these enamels may be
divided into two groups, in both of which the basis of
the design is triquetral. In the first group the pattern
may be arranged in one of two ways; its tripartite appearance is determined either by the enamelled field or
by the reserved lines which bound three fields of enamel.
The escutcheon from Kingston Down, Grave 76,[1] Kent,
and one of those from Stoke Golding, Leicestershire,[2]
show the former treatment (pl. III. 1 and 2); while the
second appears on the other Stoke Golding disk (pl. III. 3),
and in more elaborate form with the scrolls expanding
into more graceful, swelling curves on the bowl from
Lowbury Hill, Berkshire,[3] on disks from Barrington,
Cambridgeshire (Ashmolean Museum, Evans Collection, pl. III. 4), and Oving, Buckinghamshire,[4] and on
the escutcheons of the Winchester bowl.

These, along with others to be examined shortly, have
been included by Mr. Kendrick in a class which he
styles the 'Developed Trumpet Pattern', and he has put
forward the brilliant suggestion that behind the decoration of the whole class lies the classical pelta, primarily
arranged so as to form a series of linked scrolls.

The pelta might with some exercise of the imagination
be detected in the treatment of the scrolls of some of
the above pieces, where the scrolls are not actually
joined at the centre, but it seems more probable that the

[1] Bryan Faussett, *Inventorium Sepulchrale*, lv, pl. XVI. 5.
[2] *Ant. Journ.* xii. 174–5, fig., right-hand example.
[3] D. Atkinson, *Lowbury*, 21, fig. 9 and pl. v.
[4] *V.C.H., Bucks.*, i. 195, fig.

ornamentation of this sub-group was in reality influenced by, rather than created from, the pelta-motive.

But alongside this treatment there is another in which pelta-like scrolls were set on edge in reference to the circumference of the disk, in such a manner that the three could be interlocked at the centre of the design. As this treatment occurs on the Lullingstone bowl within a key-pattern border it becomes evident that it is part and parcel of the motives employed by the same general school of craftsmen as produced other works with a more classical flavour. The escutcheons thus ornamented form the largest group of all; Lullingstone[1] (and probably also Keythorpe Hall, Tugby, Leicestershire,[2] since in other respects it must come very close to the Lullingstone specimen); Camerton (a variant with a plain circle at the centre to which the arms of the design are linked); Greenwich (pl. III. 5), Middleton Moor; Hitchin; and another from an unknown source also in the Victoria and Albert Museum; from near Oxford (Pitt-Rivers Museum, Farnham, Dorset) and Chesterton-on-Fosseway, Warwickshire.

By increasing the number of scrolls to six from three, the result is the elaborate decoration of the disk in the British Museum (formerly in the Crosthwaite Museum at Keswick, but otherwise of unknown provenance), a result which has been attempted on the Winchester bowl, but without the same geometrical precision.

A few words on the matter of the enamels. The commonest colour is red, but yellow is not unknown; the disks from Barrington (pl. III. 4) and Camerton are

---

[1] G. Baldwin Brown, *The Arts in Early England*, iv. 476, pl. cxx; *Antiquity*, vi. 171, pl. IV.
[2] *Arch. Journ.* xviii. 76.

scale in inches

0   1   2

III. ENAMELLED ESCUTCHEONS

1, Kingston Down, Kent; 2, 3, Stoke Golding, Leics.;
4, Barrington, Cambs.; 5, Greenwich, Kent;
6, Hitchin, Herts.; 7, nr. Oxford

entirely in that colour. On one of the specimens from Hitchin the central part of the design is yellow, the rest is red (pl. III. 6), but in the process of firing the red seems to have come in contact with the yellow and being the stronger colour has tinged it or almost replaced it, with the result that the division of the centre from the rest is not exact at all points. The Pitt-Rivers Museum disk (pl. III. 7) is mainly red, but has spots of blue dotted about in the enamel fields, and in addition has the tail of the pelta-motive coloured yellow, as also the tips of the scrolls where they interlock with one another. Finally, on those from Oving the main design is carried out in red, but is interspersed with yellow spots.

For the moment let us turn to the genesis of the motive which constitutes the most impressive characteristic of this group. Mr. Kendrick's suggestion that behind the whole or at least the great part of the group lies the pelta must, I feel, win universal acceptance. Where I think it is possible that all will not agree with him is in his assumption of a Romanizing school to explain the excellence of the craftsmanship displayed in these enamels. The Ultimate la Tène group, as he rightly observes, is 'resolutely Celtic', and I venture to think that the southern school is, if anything, even better entitled to this designation. For the southern natives had more adverse conditions against which to contend at the outset. They could not, like their northern brethren, shake themselves free at once from the influences under which they had lived for nearly 400 years. At first they were bound on the wheel of classical tradition, and this appears not only on such pieces as those from Dover and Mildenhall already mentioned, but in others also where a quadripartite treatment of the design is employed. The Morden fragment in the British Museum shows the four peltae of the Wilton bowl executed as an enamelled disk; examples from Faversham[1] are imbued with the same principle. Even where the scroll comes to full flower, now and again the same quadripartite treatment persists, as on the poorly conceived piece from Barrington[2] or on that other from Chesterton-on-Fosseway.[3] Slowly, however, the Celtic spirit shakes itself free from its trammels. An instance of its efforts is illustrated by the Lullingstone escutcheon with its combination of a triple scroll within a key-border.

Of one thing we can rest assured, for the very course of its history proves its certainty beyond all doubt. The craft of enamelling in Britain had been, and still remained, a speciality of the Celt. In that field the Briton had nothing, as Philostratus testified, to learn from his Roman masters. The positions of master and pupil were here reversed, but, so long as the Briton was politically subject, his freedom of expression was circumscribed, and his best efforts bear the stamp of a dictated ornament. But how quickly it passes. In all the large number of escutcheons preserved to us only a small proportion shows the remotest resemblance to classical designs, and these are mere reminiscences of the past.

The Celt breaks away, free to bring his inherent ingenuity in the treatment of curvilinear patterns into play once more. We do not know fully as yet in which order the designs should be placed; their association with other objects is too imperfect as evidence. But on

---

[1] *Antiquity*, vi. 172, fig. 7, no. 1 and pl. iii.
[2] Loc. cit., fig. 7, no. 4.   [3] J. Romilly Allen, *Celtic Art*, 168.

the evidence of the subsequent history of the Celtic scroll Mr. Kendrick has offered some important and useful ideas. Following him, what do we find? Firstly, that the Celt transformed a formalized Roman grouping into a scheme whose ingenuity and liveliness arouses universal admiration. The process by which the coils of the pelta are linked together round the periphery of the disk, one only made possible by duplication of the lines of the constituent elements, and subsequently by triplication to admit of their being linked together also at the centre in an unending design, is nothing short of a triumph.[1] But side by side with these we have examples which in my opinion have nothing to do with the pelta at all; they are purely scrolled work, three coils (e.g. Stoke Golding, Leicestershire[2]) arranged round the circumference of the disk. These are purely Celtic; alike in their conception and in their treatment there is not a trace of Romanizing work, and it is these that give the clue to the trend which decorative art of this period was undergoing.

The Celt was coming into his own again. He was doing what he had done centuries before. He was participating in the creation of a fresh outburst of the Celtic artistic genius. True it is, he was taking some new models, but it is none the less a renaissance, a renaissance not of a mere system of ornament, but of the life-force which informed that ornament. This comes

[1] It is rather the actual treatment than the idea in itself that is the novelty, since this is to be seen, for instance, on a small embossed bronze plate from Hod Hill, datable either immediately before or after the Roman conquest (O. G. S. Crawford and A. Keiller, *Wessex from the Air*, fig. 3 o), or carved on the wooden plaque from Lochlee Crannog, Ayrshire (R. Munro, *Ancient Scottish Lake Dwellings or Crannogs*, 133, fig. 149).

[2] *Ant. Journ.* xii. 175.

out in nothing more clearly than the fact that at once the Celt casts aside the formal quadripartite arrangement of the design and returns to his beloved tripartite scheme, which from the first may be said to constitute the hall-mark of Celtic decoration. This is the basis on which the revival of Celtic ornament was built up; it is this which endows it with its most admirable qualities.

Here we must turn to examine its bearing on the history of the period to which this revival belongs. One or two important facts have to be taken into consideration. Firstly, all the evidence of association we possess is from the discovery of these escutcheons in graves of the early Anglo-Saxon period from A.D. 450 to 650, and in most cases rather on the late side. Examples have been found more than once in the graves of warriors, associated with a shield-boss, exaggeratedly conical in form, which Mr. Kendrick holds was developed from a type in vogue during the early period of the settlements; others come from graves in Kent, which certainly are not early, like that which contained the famous Kingston brooch; others, earlier detached from the bowl to which they had belonged, from a girl's grave so far west as Somerset.

The second fact to be noted is their distribution. This was a point which impressed itself upon me forcibly from the outset of my examination of the series, and, as I discovered later, it had struck Mr. Kendrick as equally important. Exclusive of the few stray examples found in the north, practically all have come to light within an area bounded on the west by the line of the Fosse Way. Even the exceptions from Derbyshire, in any case only a very short distance outside that line, come from within the area covered by the sphere of the

Anglo-Saxon settlements of the pagan period, as vouched for by their cemeteries. This distribution can hardly be due to mere chance.

Had this class of enamels been of more widespread manufacture, they could not have failed to come to light in other parts of the country. But the fact remains that, apart from the few specimens which I have attributed to the northern school, the entire series is focused on south-eastern England, and so far as can be judged on a point not far from London itself. This after all is the centre from which many of the earliest efforts in British enamel emanated, and maybe many of the outstanding products of that craft in Roman times.

But when were these later enamels made? Mr. Kendrick suggests that they date prior to the Anglo-Saxon conquest and belong to the fifth century, and that in most cases they were looted from native houses, or, if their sacral character be admitted, from churches of the pre-Saxon natives, by the invaders. That seems to be the most probable explanation, especially as the history of the bowls which they serve to decorate can be traced back to pre-Saxon times.

Another explanation has been suggested to me by Mr. A. W. Clapham, namely that, if their distribution and association can be said to argue anything, it is that they were made by native craftsmen to the order of their new masters, the Anglo-Saxons, to whom the mystery of enamelling was a sealed book, and to whom the richness of the colouring and the novelty of the designs might well prove attractive. In short, the distribution coinciding with that of the early Anglo-Saxon settlements proves that, since their association indicates that they need not in most cases have been made before the period of the invasions, they must have been made after the invasion. Seeing, however, that during the initial period of the invasions the natives would have been far too occupied with other more serious affairs to have had leisure for the luxury crafts of peace, they could hardly have been made before the later sixth or seventh century.

It has more than once in the past been maintained that the art of these enamels was generated from an Irish source. But how should this be? Firstly, we have their counterpart in purely classical designs, such as never appear in Ireland and apparently belonging to the same general period, though not all these works in enamel need be absolutely contemporaneous. Secondly, not a single example has ever been found in Ireland.

There is yet another argument against such a theory, even though it is of a negative character. During the period of the Viking raids in Ireland, the invaders looted large quantities of Irish metal-work and carried it back to Scandinavia, but there were still large enough quantities left behind to enrich the Irish museums at the present day. Among these there is a plenty of examples of the Ultimate la Tène style in metal. But in spite of the existence of the Book of Durrow and the Book of Kells, not a single piece of metal-work, antecedent in date, is known from Irish soil that repeats the scroll-patterns of those and other later manuscripts. All the other periods are richly represented; only the one essential to support the theory is wanting. In England, on the other hand, it is the manuscripts that are missing. They were more perishable. The more durable metal-work has survived, and this, in view of the wealth of metallic evidence of all other periods of Irish art, should have also survived in Ireland, had it ever existed there. It is to be remembered that we do not know, and indeed may never know, what impulse gave rise to the origins of the Irish manuscripts. For even the Ultimate la Tène style seems more than probably to have been a product of northern England and southern Scotland, and in any case belongs to an art-province that comprises these areas and north-eastern Ireland.

What then is the corollary of this amazing reappearance of a Celtic ornament in Britain? In using the word Celtic here I anticipate the point at which my road diverges from that taken by Mr. Kendrick. The date of these escutcheons precludes the derivation of their ornamental motives from the actual designs that were employed in the illumination of the Book of Durrow, for which no earlier date than the close of the seventh century is now admitted even if such had been suggested. Meagre though the material evidence at our disposal be, does it not imply that this renaissance started in England, and that the flight of the natives before the devastation and massacre by the invaders, of which Gildas has drawn so poignant a picture, carried the art overseas to Ireland, where once more it was able to work and develop free from molestation and the turmoil of war.[1] Other evidence, indeed, exists to show that this hypothesis is in consonance with the actual facts. Mr. Regi-

---

[1] It is here, I think, that Mr. Clapham's suggestion encounters a serious obstacle. The art of the escutcheons is purely native; they appear only in the area occupied by the Anglo-Saxons; they have never been found in Celtic Wales, and only sporadically and in a variant style in northern England. If made to the order of the invaders, it could only be at a time when the country had sunk back again to a fair degree of peace; and one would reasonably expect that the art would then have spread to all parts of the country, especially to more Celtic districts, and even have found its way to Ireland in the sixth or early seventh century, while at the same time persisting in eastern Britain as well.

nald Smith in a paper on the development of the Irish
ring-brooch, of which the so-called Tara brooch is a
notable example, points out that the form can be traced
back to one which has been found in Saxon graves, for
example in Sussex.[1] Its ancestry, indeed, goes back to
early Celtic times in Britain, and, as he shows, the subsequent stages of its evolution are to be seen in examples
found in Wales; and further, none of the early types
occur in Ireland. The evidence is scanty, but it is there,
and calls for the most serious consideration.

This brings us to that most wonderful manifestation
of Celtic art, the illuminated manuscripts and their
contemporary products. For long enough it has been
held that England owed many of its manuscripts and
certainly all its inspiration to the skill of Irish craftsmen,
and that it was only through the influence of Irish monks
that the English monasteries acquired the knowledge
which enabled them to develop a school or schools of
their own. I know that here I am treading a thorny
path, but I say with all the deliberation which so serious
a problem demands that a school of thought exists
which has long suspected, and is now rapidly confirming
its suspicion, that the role played by England in this
matter has been grossly under-estimated, and that
England has at least as many claims to the parentage of
the art of illumination, as practised in the British Isles
in the eighth to tenth centuries, as Ireland.

The scroll-motives of the Book of Durrow were
known in England at least a century, possibly two, and
conceivably still longer before they can be dated in
Ireland, and we know for a fact that many of the animal

---

[1] *Archaeologia*, lxv. 226; the form occurred in a fourth century
context at Traprain Law (*Proc. Soc. Ant. Scot.*, liv. 88, fig. 19, no. 1).

motives which adorn the manuscripts were borrowed from the Teutonic zoomorphic ornament, as Salin,[1] in whom protohistoric research has lost a brilliant exponent, demonstrated many years ago. I may perhaps be permitted to make a small contribution to his thesis.

The escutcheons found in an Anglian grave at Benty Grange, Derbyshire, have long been known to bear animal forms. The presence of an imperfect example from the set in the Ashmolean Museum has allowed me an opportunity of studying it in detail, and from that fragment it has been possible to complete a restoration of the design (fig. 40).[2] At once we detect not only its

FIG. 40. Restoration of enamelled escutcheon from Benty Grange, Derbyshire ([1]). [The dark portions are original.]

close resemblance to the biting animals on the sword-pommel from Kent cited by Salin, but one even closer to the row of biting animals in the Book of Durrow. Indeed the design has much more in common with animals of a non-Anglo-Saxon type. They are in fact the fishes which appear on the escutcheons from Faversham in the British Museum, here arranged in a circular design, and in feeling they offer perhaps a better parallel to the animals in the Book of Durrow than does the pair on the Kentish pommel. One more point in this connexion. A further fragment from the same grave at

[1] B. Salin, *Die Altgermanische Thierornamentik*, 339.
[2] This is probably more accurate than Mr. Kendrick's figure which was based on the still less perfect example in Sheffield Museum.

Benty Grange and preserved along with that decorated
with animal-ornament can be clearly seen to belong to
an entirely different motive, nothing less, in short, than
the scroll-designs which are the predominant motives
employed upon the escutcheons in England. Thus, at
Benty Grange we meet already in combination two of
the elements that go to make up the Book of Durrow.
As for the plait-work, Zimmerman may be perfectly
correct in believing that it came from the Near East.
We have evidence, as Sir Martin Conway has shown,
that objects of Coptic fabric were finding their way to
Saxon England, but we have nevertheless guilloche
designs of two strands occurring on Saxon brooches.[1]
The plait-motive can well have survived with all the
other ingredients of Celtic art. It occurs too commonly
on mosaic floors in this country for it not to have been
familiar to native artists without further borrowing from
abroad. The two-strand and three-strand distinction
seems to be overlaboured.

The long and short of the whole matter seems to be
that behind the whole series of metal-work and illumination that forms so remarkable a feature of Christian Celtic art there lies, what was in the nature of the
case inevitable, a period of experiment and trial. It can
hardly be Roman, pure and simple, for it has no exact
counterpart abroad. It must, therefore, be an outburst
of artistic expression on the part of a people left to their

[1] e.g. W. M. Wylie, *Fairford Graves*, pl. III. 4; *Proc. Soc. Ant.* iv.
28, fig.; *Archaeologia*, lxiii. 164–5, figs. 5 and 6, pl. XXV, and pl. XXVI. 3.
How much the Saxon and Romano-Briton were interlocked within
quite a short time is demonstrated by the frequency of classical designs
in Anglo-Saxon work of the later pagan period, in borders of egg and
tongue, guilloche, and tendril. An excellent example of the last is the
brooch from Alfriston, Sussex (G. Baldwin Brown, *The Arts in Early
England*, iii. 304, pl. LII. 11, a treatment essentially non-Teutonic).

own devices once more. As Mr. Kendrick very justly observes, much of it must be assigned to the efforts of a people long inured to classical art, endeavouring to preserve the lessons of the preceding three and a half centuries. Their efforts, as shown above, seem to have survived right down into Saxon times, for the classical patterns I have mentioned are common in the Saxon districts, Sussex and Wessex. The natives were on equal terms with the Saxons, even though the latter came in all the fresh vigour of invasion; the canons on which the former were working were foreign to the Saxon both in their conception and their application. If the new-comers were to succeed at all, they must be prepared to receive that infusion of insular feeling to which all artistic canons introduced into these islands have had to submit. During the Roman period we see the constant recrudescence of Celtic traits. *Naturam expellas furca, tamen usque recurret*, but conditions under Roman rule gave it no real liberty of action. When Britain was finally left by Rome to its own fate, it had been too long under foreign tutelage to be able at first to shake off the torpor of an imposed foreign art; its creative power was dulled, its individuality blunted. On the top of this it had almost at once to face another invasion to which it had little power to offer an effectual resistance.

We have yet to learn whether the new style began before the Saxon invasion or after. In the second event, all that need be said is that the wild freedom of Teutonic art was more akin to the native spirit than the ordered formalism of classical art, and so a sympathy of artistic ideas diminished the paralysing stress of invasion.

But in both events, if we seek to learn a lesson from

the art of the escutcheons, the one fact that emerges
more clearly than all is that no ornamental system could
prevail until it could be rendered congenial to native
taste, and that is essentially what took place in this
obscure period. It has been maintained that the background of Christian Celtic art, as it appears after A.D. 700,
is to be sought in a Romanizing school, and if this
means that the impulses towards the revival seem to
have sprung forth in the more Romanized districts of
Britain, I follow the same road. But beyond that point
my way parts.

In any case no Christianizing art could neglect ideas
derived from classical sources, and an essential feature
of the Romanizing school is the principle of four-square,
quadripartite arrangement. It is, however, not this,
but the tripartite principle, so beloved of the Celts from
the time of their first efforts of the la Tène epoch and
preserved intact by them throughout the Roman period,
that finally prevails. Just as on the Rhine and in Gaul
the Celts had earlier taken the motives of classical
Greece and Rome and shaped them to their aesthetic
needs, so did the natives in Britain gather up the leavings
of Roman art in Britain, and by the infection of their
own spirit transmute them into a very living thing.

The distinction between the treble and double plait
has, I maintain, been overlaboured. The two actually
appear side by side on the Lullingstone bowl, and it
may well be that the example of zoomorphic ornament
which in its more advanced stage interlaces two contour
lines was not without influence on the number of lines
employed. Whether in the scrolls, the plait-work, or the
zoomorphic designs the unfailing genius of the craftsmen in the British Isles for moulding borrowed motives

into a national style comes to the fore, and it is evident
from what has come down from the early Anglo-Saxon
period that once the settlements were firmly established
the process set in once more. But, even if we admit that
some of the motives that go to make up the style of
Christian Celtic art from the seventh century onwards
were borrowed from continental sources, we are still
confronted by a phenomenon as yet unexplained,
namely, how from the very first the artists evolved the
perfectly amazing ingenuity in the arrangement of their
plait-work, so fully described by Romilly Allen. No
European art can offer anything in the slightest degree
equivalent. In any case the constituent elements which
we find in due course in Christian Celtic art can all in
a greater or lesser degree be discovered among the
motives current in Britain, possibly in the fifth, certainly
in the sixth and seventh centuries. As known to us they
are at a more or less tentative stage. That may be due
to the absence of objects with large surfaces on which,
as on the manuscripts, they might have been employed.
We possess, fortunately, another criterion which tells
us that the interpretation of this scanty material is the
right one, namely the enamels of the escutcheons. For
these, as we have seen, are not confined to single colours,
red or yellow alone. On some examples more ambitious
schemes have been successfully attempted. From a
blend of a yellow centre in an otherwise red field on a
Hitchin escutcheon we pass to a more balanced distribution of the two colours on the Oving example, while on
the Farnham Museum example the addition of yellow
tips to the red scrolls is reminiscent of the manuscripts.

In short, it is in Britain, and in Britain alone—for it is
certain that nothing comparable is to be seen in Ireland

—that we must look for the seeds from which sprang many of the fairest blossoms of Celtic Christian art. There is nothing here of detraction of the work of the Irish illuminators and craftsmen. What they accomplished holds of right a very high place among the world's artistic creations. As did the Celts of Britain, so they in turn displayed that genius for adaptation which stamps the whole history of Celtic ornament in the British Isles, and with their missionary activities the Irish were able to give some of it back to the lands from which all Celtic art had sprung.

INDEXES

I. GENERAL INDEX

II. LOCALITIES

PRINTED IN
GREAT BRITAIN
AT THE
UNIVERSITY PRESS
OXFORD
BY
JOHN JOHNSON
PRINTER
TO THE
UNIVERSITY